Trips and Trails, 2

**Family Camps, Short Hikes and View Roads
in the Olympics, Mt. Rainier and South Cascades**

Third Edition

Text: E.M. Sterling
Photos: Bob and Ira Spring

THE MOUNTAINEERS • SEATTLE

THE MOUNTAINEERS: Organized 1906
"...to explore, study, preserve and enjoy
the natural beauty of Northwest America."

First printing, June 1968
Second printing, August 1970
Third printing, August 1972
Revised, 1974
Second edition, first printing, August 1977; second printing, September 1979
Third edition, first printing, March 1983; second printing, May 1984

Published by The Mountaineers
715 Pike St., Seattle, Washington 98101

Published simultaneously in Canada by Douglas & McIntyre, Ltd.
1615 Venables Street, Vancouver, British Columbia V5L 2H1

Manufactured in the United States of America

Maps by Marge Mueller and Helen Sherman
Book design by Marge Mueller
Cover photo: Takhlakh Lake reflects 12,326-ft. Mt. Adams, Gifford Pinchot National Forest

Library of Congress Cataloging in Publication Data

Sterling, E. M.
    Trips and trails.

    Includes bibliographical references.
    Contents: —v. 2. Family camps, short hikes,
and view roads in the Olympics, Mt. Rainier, and South
Cascades.
    1. Hiking—Washington (State)—Guide-books.
2. Camp sites, facilities, etc.—Washington (State)—
Guide-books.   3. Family recreation—Washington (State)
—Guide-books.   4. Washington (State)—Description and
travel—1981- —Guide-books.   I. Spring, Bob,
1918-   . II. Spring, Ira. III. Title.
GV199.42.W2S75   1983   917.97'5   83-2253
ISBN 0-89886-069-5 (v. 2)

CONTENTS

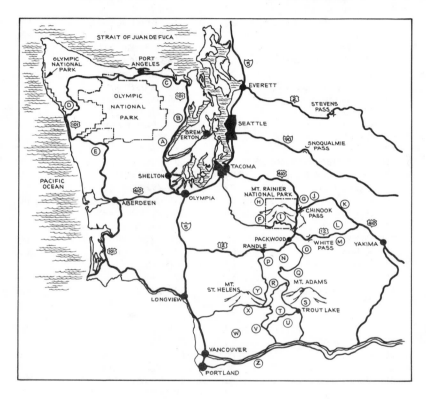

FOREWORD

Among the titles proposed for this book was **Lazy Man's Guide to Mountain Recreation,** to suggest that one need not be a daring climber or steel-muscled backwoodsman to enjoy the Alpine Lakes, Mt. Rainier, and other portions of the central and south Cascades. The idea was rejected because it conjured up the tourist who rarely gets out of the car and when he does keeps one hand on the door, and the camper who stakes out a homestead in a campground and for the whole weekend never leaves the quadrilateral bounded by trailer, picnic table, water faucet, and privy.

The implied emphasis in the title finally chosen is on trips and trails **from** campgrounds (though many can equally well be done in a day from the city). The book is designed to lead **away** from the camp and into the woods, along the trails, and beside the rivers, and up from well-traveled main roads onto lonesome roads with views and walks and things to do. Campgrounds are described, and the author surveys the theory and practice of "light camping" (as opposed to the expensive, equipment-overburdened, mechanized variety), but the theme of the book is that while camping is good fun, it's even more fun to go snooping around.

The country covered is for everyone. Lack of outdoor experience is no barrier. Fresh from the sidewalks of New York or the tall corn of Iowa, one can enjoy these trips and trails to mountains and rivers. Nor is age a barrier. Often one hears a mother or father with small children say, "We'd like to get out, and we will when the kids are older." In fact, the average child 2 or 3 can manage several miles a day under his own power—more with an occasional piggyback ride—and have a grand time splashing in puddles, peering at beetles.

The Philosophy of Anti-City

Cities are necessary devices, but conveniences and pleasures fitting in a city may be nuisances or even crudities in the outback. Unfortunately, too many people fail to distinguish between city and non-city. Attracted to mountains and beaches by the elemental simplicity, they yet insist on burdening themselves with luxuries and paraphernalia and gadgetry and noisemakers and impedimenta of the subdivision and freeway.

A refinement of taste is needed. People who like both city and back country must face up to their schizophrenia and separate their two lives.

The well-adjusted, thoughtful person who has completed a full self-analysis consciously **does not** carry the city into the wilds. For example, in the campground he does not abolish night by hanging a gasoline lantern to a tree, but instead enjoys the flames and coals of the campfire, enjoys the moon and stars, enjoys the darkness.

Camper-trucks and to a lesser extent trailers have their place. But those who seal themselves into portable subdivisions come evening or a sprinkle of rain miss the sound of the river, the brush of the wind, the smell of the trees. They leave at home the telephone and TV; the radio they have along, turned on loud to drown out the owls.

For some, the escape from the city is a chance to shed inhibitions. Sedate gentlemen, pillars of the community, do things in the hills they would never dare at home. They lash scooters to their trailers or campers, and once at the campground razz around like squirrels in a cage. The gutsy ones challenge the trails, sublimating frustrations of inadequate childhoods.

The scooter (motorized trail bike) is no worse than the automobile, and in truth is not as bad by far—two wheels less, two tons less. Cities will be better off when people move about with a minimum of metal and fossil-fuel consumption. Scooters are also excellent for back roads, including (in Washington State) thousands of miles of tracks impassable or uncomfortable for automobiles. Scooters should be encouraged on roads and rough tracks (as well as on city streets) as a partial solution to the automobile problem.

However, it is an article of faith here that machines are inappropriate and antisocial—and above all in **bad taste**—on traditional foot trails. The National Park

Service agrees and bans scooters absolutely from paths. The U.S. Forest Service, hung up on the horns of the "multiple-use" dilemma, bars scooters from a few trails but complacently accepts them on most, and indeed is rebuilding many to allow wheeled travel.

The philosophy of anti-city dictates that all traditional foot trails, everywhere, be closed to machinery of every kind. As the gasoline lantern pollutes night, the infernal combustion engine pollutes quiet.

An ideal might be stated that expresses the motivation of this book: when visiting the back country to camp and hike and prowl, **take along just as little of the city as you can.** Camp as light as you can. Walk as much as you can. Be as dark at night, and as quiet night and day, as you can. On road, trail, campground, be as clean as you can, carrying garbage home rather than leaving it scattered about as your "sign."

Mt. Rainier

One would think the grandest physical object in the contiguous 48 states, recognized in 1899 as America's fourth national park, would be entirely within the park, from summit snows to forested base; it is not.

One might imagine the Forest Service, finding itself the accidental custodian of some flanks and valleys, would treat The Mountain with special respect; it has not. Recently, Forest Service logging roads have been gouged high onto buttressing ridges near the Carbon River and the West Fork of the White River; around the Mowich River and the North Fork Puyallup, private heirs of the notorious Northern Pacific Land Grant are involved.

Conservationists are supporting an omnibus statewide wilderness bill known as the Washington Wilderness Bill. This bill includes wilderness protection for the Tatoosh Range to the south of the park and the Clearwater area to the north of the park. This area features some of the few old growth forest still untouched in the state and also includes alpine meadows and lakes that would be a logical complement to the park. These additions would preserve some of the forest as well as the glaciated peak.

Cougar Lakes

Bordering Mt. Rainier National Park on the east, atop and beyond the Cascade Crest, lies a valley-and-alpine wildland that could and should provide breathing room for the overcrowded, underprotected mountain. Preservationists propose a Cougar Lakes Wilderness Area to do just that.

The Forest Service proposes, instead, a miniscule Mt. Aix Wilderness limited to summit rocks, and would log the valleys and build roads into meadows so delicate they can scarcely tolerate even the present hiking and horse-riding traffic.

Compounding the threat, the U.S. Bureau of Reclamation wants to enlarge Bumping Lake with a new dam—more trees cut, more river bottom turned into mudhole. Since the Bureau has been unable to justify the dam on the basis of supplying irrigation water (which opponents have proven can be obtained elsewhere), it has tried to sweeten the benefit-cost ratio with recreation—more reservoir recreation, of which Washington and the Northwest already have a plethora.

Conservationists support the Cougar Lakes Wilderness as part of the Washington Wilderness Bill. The north unit with 67,000 acres straddles the Cascade Crest from Chinook Pass north to Naches Pass. This area includes Norse Peak, Crow Basin, and the low elevation valleys of the Upper Greenwater and the Little Naches Rivers. The south unit, comprising about 190,000 acres, stretches from Chinook Pass south to White Pass along the eastern boundary of Mt. Rainier National Park. To the southwest the meadows and innumerable lakes of the unique Tumac Plateau are readily accessible for backcountry travelers of all ages. Eastward the dryer and more rugged ridges provide solitude. Both Mt. Aix and Bismarck Creek tower over the several forks of Rattlesnake Creek. Breathtaking hikes are rewarded with panoramic views of pristine countryside. American Ridge and the Cougar Lakes themselves to the north provide additional variety and spectacular scenery.

Mt. Adams and Goat Rocks

If there weren't a Mt. Rainier, Mt. Adams would have been a national park in 1899. Because there is a Rainier, Adams is treated as a surplus volcano. A quarter-century ago the Forest Service (aiming to put to rest once and for all a splendid proposal for an Ice Peaks National Park that would have included all the Cascade volcanoes, from the Columbia River to Canada) established a Mt. Adams Wild Area extending from the summit icecap to just a bit below the moraines. It also set aside the adjacent Goat Rocks Wild Area, noted (before shooting resumed after years of protection) for extraordinarily large numbers of mountain goat. (Despite preposterous claims of the Washington State Game Department that the population is stable, goats in fact are disappearing fast.)

With the Forest Service's propensity for road building, too much has happened under its management to reconstitute the wilderness that might have been. However, a wide belt of public lands surrounding the wild cores could be placed in a Mt. Adams and Goat Rocks Recreation Area, halting the continuing multiple-abuse degradation. And the "hoofed locusts," as John Muir called sheep, could be barred from the high country, where now a hiker often may go for miles through the stinking wreckage of chewed flowers, never daring drink the polluted water running from the snows. The Mt. Adams Additions, which are part of the Washington Wilderness Bill, provide additional protection for the wilderness as well as offering suitable lowland recreation.

St. Helens

Had a geologic miracle erupted St. Helens in New Jersey or Illinois, it would have become the first national park, long before Yellowstone. In the volcano-overpopulated Cascades it offers a good (bad) example of the Forest Service mismanagement of scenery.

After the eruption of St. Helens in 1980, various proposals were developed to protect the unique area created by the eruption. Conservationists supported a proposal for a 216,000-acre Monument. In 1982 Congress passed legislation creating a 110,000-acre National Volcanic Monument. The Monument will contain areas for scientific study and recreational use in the area affected by the blast, old growth forest in parts of the Green River and Goat Creek areas, and the Kipuka Lava Flow. The Monument will be managed by the Forest Service under management guidelines contained in the legislation. Although the Monument does not protect all of the area proposed by conservationists, it will protect areas of great scientific, historic and recreational interest.

The Monument was only one of the many critical Wilderness proposals incorporated in the Washington Wilderness Bill. Congress has all the information it needs to act on this bill. What Congress needs is to see the light and feel the heat, and that is where your letters, telephone calls, and personal contacts will make the difference.

About The Mountaineers

The Mountaineers, with groups based in Seattle, Everett, Tacoma, and Olympia, invite the membership of all lovers of outdoor life who sympathize with the purposes of the organization and wish to share in its activities.

The above brief and partial summary of Mountaineer concerns in the central and south Cascades (in other areas are other concerns) suggests the importance of the club role in conservation education and action. If you share these concerns, your membership is particularly desired and needed.

Preservation, though, is only one side of the coin; the other is using and enjoying the back country.

The Mountaineers sponsor a year-round program of climbing, hiking, camping, ski-touring, and snowshoeing. Hundreds of outings are scheduled each year, ranging

Sea stacks at Second Beach

from single-day walks to trips lasting 2 weeks or more. On a typical weekend as many as 20 or 30 excursions may be offered, from ocean beaches to the summit of Mt. Rainier. In addition, members engage in countless privately-organized trips of all kinds; perhaps a major value in belonging to an outdoor organization (The Mountaineers or any other) is the opportunity to meet other people with similar interests, to make new friends.

For further information on club activities and how to join, write The Mountaineers, 719 Pike St., Seattle, Washington 98101.

THE MOUNTAINEERS

INTRODUCTION

Camping, as defined in these books, has very little to do with tents, sleeping bags, or stoves. Camping, as we mean it here, is simply a method of reaching the edge of adventure, of escaping from the rigors of the city into the boundless freedom of the outdoors. And it's the same too with the hiking outlined here. No labor is intended. We list our hikes in the tradition of Robert Louis Stevenson and Thoreau—great hikers both—as journeys, jaunts, and strolls designed for temperate walkers who hike, not just to walk, but to understand and see.

No trail here, therefore, should be rushed or lunged at. All should be dawdled over, savored and enjoyed. Every creek should be played in, fallen log rested on, waterfall climbed beneath, meadow sprawled upon, and hollow tree hidden in. And all marmots must be whistled at, chipmunks talked to, and green frogs held.

"Overwalkers"—those who hike more with muscle than with soul—may discover some pleasures here. But most trips they will find too short. For the majority are well within the 3-hour limit Stevenson thought ideal; and only a few extend to the 4 hours Thoreau preferred. Most are 2 miles one way, or less, and many are shorter than a mile, round trip.

All hikes here can be solo affairs. Most walkers of the past preferred to stroll alone, seeking privacy on the road to argue, sing, and ruminate to themselves. But our selection is designed mostly for family treks. Not that privacy isn't possible on such hikes. Children often seem to enjoy not hearing from their parents as much as parents enjoy not hearing sounds their offspring make.

On family hikes, however, organized loitering must supplant the solo pace. Each person must allow all others to see those things that excite them most.

Big rocks that can be climbed on, crooked trees, toads, and funny-looking stones hold more attraction to a boy than a sweeping vista or pluming waterfalls his mother might enjoy. But on these mountain trails there's room for both. So if you hike—and it's our devout hope that you will—let boys jump, girls brood, wives rest, and husbands pontificate as each is wont. Let every person find his private secret; let no one question his right to seek it out.

All trails described should normally be easy to find and stay on. Most are clearly marked and signed, although logging and logging road changes sometimes disrupt them all. Very few of the goals listed here demand cross-country hiking. Those that do are clearly identified. A novice should always turn back any time he feels the route unsafe.

No special equipment will be required for any hikes spelled out here. Hiking boots with rubber-lugged soles, the kind sold at mountaineer equipment stores, will make all hikes more enjoyable. For trails abound with mud, roots, rocks, snow, and rain-sopped brush, sometimes all at once. (And that's the way they should be.) Tennis shoes, however, will suffice to start.

Hikers should always carry what The Mountaineers consider the "Ten Essentials"—sunglasses, knife, matches, firestarter, first aid kit, flashlight, compass, a map, extra clothing (particularly if you start out in shorts and T-shirt and head for stormy altitudes), and extra food—all carried in a rucksack "just in case."

Newcomers shouldn't overlook the opportunities many of the suggested trails offer for an overnight "test" backpack trip. A short hike offers a chance to shake down backpacking equipment and practice the discipline of stowing and deleting gear without the high risk of failure inherent in a longer, more arduous trip.

CAMPING

As we indicated, camping as defined here should have very little to do with equipment. The essence of what we mean by camping will not be found in campgrounds but along trails, streams, and logging roads, in flowers, stars,

waterfalls, vistas, and beautiful rocks — in the thrill of seeing, touching, and hearing the surprises of nature.

Some equipment, of course, is necessary. But it takes very little to start. A few pots and pans, a stove, sleeping bags, and a shelter of some sort will more than get the job done. Many novices, however, so overwhelm themselves with elaborate tents, chairs, lanterns, cushions, cots, mattresses, tables, ice chests, jugs, heaters, and even sinks they spend most of their time doing nothing but loading and unloading gear.

A new camper should buy nothing until he is certain he needs it — and probably not then. Avoid mistakes by borrowing or renting to start, buying only after you've either tried out equipment or seen others use it under campground conditions. There are no secrets to acquiring good equipment. Deal with a reputable store — preferably one dealing in mountaineering equipment. Buy standard brands at standard prices, avoiding big promotions and "sales" unless you **know** the gear is good. When in doubt, talk to other campers.

Sleeping bags filled with 3 to 4 pounds of synthetic fiber seem most popular at present. Durability of the outer covering appears to pose the biggest choice factor. Down-filled bags remain the best, but unless a family expects to do extensive backpacking the lighter weight is seldom worth the much higher price.

Mattresses range from lightweight plastic- or rubber-foam pads to conventional air mattresses. The pads range from 4 to 6 inches in thickness for car-camping with much thinner ones offered for backpacking. Fabric-type air mattresses are more durable than those of purely plastic design.

A **camp stove** has become virtually indispensable as the supply of firewood in and around campgrounds diminishes. Never base meal plans on a campfire alone. The two-burner pump-type stoves are popular. But the compact backpacker-types offered at mountaineer, alpine, and recreational equipment stores are much preferred by many.

The **tent** is the most expensive item in a camping outfit and perhaps the least essential. Actually, all the average camper does there is sleep. Many campers find plastic tarps sufficient protection and use nothing else. Most campers, however, eventually end up with a tent for the sake of privacy in crowded areas, and as protection from wind in higher camps.

Tents come in all shapes and sizes. Again, buy what you want from a reputable equipment store after considering such matters as ease in setting it up, size, stability in the wind, weight, bulk, and, of course, price.

Other equipment such as tarps, lanterns, ice chests, gas and water cans, ovens, chairs, axes and saws, etc., should be purchased only after the need arises — if then. All campers carry some extras. But the competency of the camper and the amount of time he spends away from his equipment enjoying "camping" invariably can be measured by how few.

Pots, Pans, and Menus

Cooks face the most difficult equipment-paring job of all. City-type cooking takes all sorts of equipment, as any household kitchen proves.

Obviously, it can't all be hauled to camp. Picking the right items can certainly be difficult. But the cook who wants to partake in the pleasures of camping — and cooking and dishwashing do not qualify — will get the job done. Experienced camp cooks have done it. A novice will find a way.

First of all, campers have no right to expect fancy meals in the woods — even if they get them. Whims of the city should be left there. Finicky children should be ignored. The desires of the cook come first. And no one should go camping just to eat, anyway.

Simple menus, preplanned and packaged, can reduce cookery and equipment to a minimum. Many cooks serve the same camp meals trip in and trip out — and on paper plates too. After all, weekend camping involves only 4 meals out of the week's total of

21. The family can complain while it's home.
Select pots and pans to fit menu needs, leaving home those not needed. Camp cooks generally prefer a separate set of utensils, primarily because it's impossible to keep camping pots scoured to kitchen standards. Cooking kits are popular, but many cooks use home discards and let it go at that.

Cooking aids and staple stocks should also be chosen carefully and pared relentlessly. Brass scouring pads, cheese cloth dishtowels (they dry rapidly), fire starters, mitten potholders, can openers, a jackknife, tongs, and a couple of spoons are included in most cooking sets. Food staples should be transferred to plastic containers to save space and provide some control over items carried. Cardboard boxes get wet and glass breaks.

Clothing

Weekend trips demand very few clothes. In most instances, the ones worn from home will do. Except for rain gear, swim suits, and sweaters for chill evenings, many families carry just one set of extra clothing, hoping that only one child falls in the creek.

If you must buy clothes, don't worry about style. Comfort and service are the only requirements. Sturdy clothes from any store will do, of course. But if you're looking for clothing particularly designed and fabricated for hiking and camping, shop at mountaineering stores that specialize in such items.

Packing

A firm plan for packing and loading equipment can save time and soothe nerves on any camping trip. Each piece of equipment should be stored in the same container in the same place and loaded into the same spot in the car on each trip.

Campers use every type of container from wicker baskets through packboards to cardboard boxes (not preferred). Checklists help.

CAMPGROUNDS

Campsites here range from those in highly-developed — and overcrowded — campgrounds on main thoroughfares to primitive, undeveloped, and uncrowded spots along remote logging roads.

All formal campgrounds offer the camping basics of a parking space, tables, firepits, toilet facilities, and water from a well, creek, or lake. Fee camps provide piped water and restrooms, as extras. The fee, however, also buys crowds.

In the National Forests — and in the National Forests **only** — one may pitch camp any place. The practice is starting to cause concern as the number of people and sanitation problems grow. But it's still allowed providing the camper carries ax, shovel, and bucket for fire control.

Firewood is provided in some National Forest camps. Otherwise it must be rustled alongside mountain roads — away from camp. More sensibly, use a gas stove.

LOGGING ROADS

Logging roads are exactly what the name implies: roads designed, built, and used for logging operations. They are often rough, steep, muddy, narrow, and dusty. Many switchback endlessly. Some seem no more than penciled on cliffs. Occasionally one may be blocked by snow, slides, or fallen trees. (And this too is the way it should be. Logging roads were never designed as highways.) But all of them here can be driven safely, with care and caution, albeit in low gear, by a passenger car.

Even a blocked road, however, need not ruin a trip. One can always park and walk. A short hike often can salvage a tremendous view that would otherwise be missed.

High-altitude roads may remain closed by snow until late summer. When planning high trips through early July, it is wise to telephone ranger stations in advance for road reports. If driving logging roads in midweek, be particularly alert for logging trucks.

COURTESY

There was a time when men could do as they wanted in the campgrounds and mountain trails of the Pacific Northwest. But not anymore. There are too many people now. Each person must bend a little to the needs of those around him. Courtesy is no longer a nicety. It's imperative.

Radios. Music is lovely and news is interesting but served secondhand in a crowded campground both are a plague. If radio owners have a universal failing besides their choice of music (I like mine, but hate yours) it's their complete indifference to how far their sound penetrates a campground at night. No radio should be played after 10 p.m., a traditional camp bedtime. And the sound at other hours should not exude beyond the radio-owners' own campsite.

Lanterns. Light your own world but not that of others in the campground. Remember, the lantern that hisses and glares over your camp table also glares and hisses through the walls of **every** nearby tent. Lanterns are completely unnecessary on long, late summer evenings. But if you feel you must use one, shield its glare.

Scooters. Scooters have a place. But it most certainly is **not** in a campground or on a trail closed to motorized vehicles. Campers should have no qualms about seeking their ouster whenever they appear in such places. Scooters can be banned by regulation in all campgrounds. Some rangers and forest supervisors, however, haven't been anxious to enforce such rules, so make sure that they do. Anytime — ANYTIME — scooters appear, in any campground or on any closed trail complain about them. Insist on enforcement of the regulations.

Garbage. Not too long ago, campers and hikers were advised to bury and burn their garbage. Some publications still advise it. But don't. Garbage nowadays either should be put in a garbage can or else lugged home and disposed of there. Even in remote trail areas, campers must not drop, hide, bury, or burn their trash. Haul it all back. Some forests are now conducting haul-your-trash-back campaigns. Cooperate. Please.

Trees. If firewood is not supplied in a campground, do **not** chop your own. Many campgrounds look as if they had undergone an artillery barrage, with every tree and shrub splintered and mangled by hatchets and saws. If you must have firewood, seek it amidst windfallen limbs and snags off logging roads. Some campers haul dry wood from home.

Vandals. There is little use in urging campers to refrain from destroying campground facilities. Those who perform such acts are beyond urging. Report any vandalism you witness to authorities. Let them impose whatever punishment the law affords.

Fire. Every year, despite loud and frequent public pleas, rangers battle blazes caused by campers who have simply failed to think. In formal campgrounds confine all fire to established firepits. In primitive areas, douse all fires until the coals **feel** cool. Carry a shovel, ax, and bucket at all times.

E. M. STERLING

ACKNOWLEDGMENTS

After nature, one owes huge obligations to men in compiling a book like this.

We must start first with our families whose endless tolerance permitted the effort in the first place. Then gratitude is due generously to the many officials of Olympic and Mt. Rainier National Parks and Snoqualmie, Wenatchee, and Gifford Pinchot National Forests, who gave so willingly of their time and knowledge to introduce us to their forests and check our material for accuracy.

Nor do we confine our thanks to these alone. Every person who ever roamed these mountains played some role. For it is because of them that many of the wild spectacles still exist today, as they will exist — or not exist — tomorrow because of each of you.

E. M. STERLING
BOB AND IRA SPRING

EXPLANATION OF SYMBOLS

 Trails suitable for children up to 8. Easy and safe walking for all ages.

 Difficult trails. Safe if walked sanely and knowledgeably. But no place for uncontrolled youngsters (of any age) or persons who tire easily. Hike only in lug-soled shoes.

 Sunday-driver type roads. Mostly paved or well-graded gravel. Roads that can be driven easily by the most wary driver — young or old. Easy on new cars.

 Rough roads. Often extremely dusty on hot days and slick after rains. But none are unsafe (see introduction) providing they are driven with constant care. On some, 10 miles an hour is speeding.

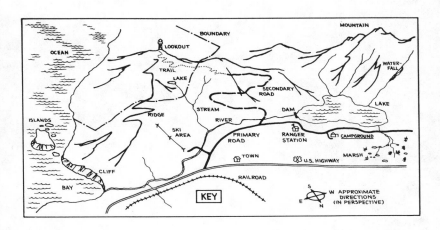

A   OLYMPIC PENINSULA

Ocean beaches, cathedral-like rain forests, sparkling lakes and spectacular high-mountain vistas. All from a single highway that loops the Olympic Peninsula.

A very popular area, this. And heavily used. But still a place where privacy can be found on trails and ocean beaches. Facilities at lower levels are open almost the year around. Inland — and higher — camps open as spring moves up the mountains.

And reaching this area can be as interesting as the visit itself. From Seattle, catch any of several ferries across Puget Sound to Bremerton, Winslow, Kingston and Port Townsend, taking Highway 101 north or south to the many recreation spots around the peninsula loop. Or drive from Seattle south to Olympia and then on to the Pacific Ocean coast or north to the Strait of Juan de Fuca.

The east side of the peninsula offers camping along Hood Canal or in the foothills of the Olympics. The northern section offers clear lakes and high vistas, some with views that stretch from the ocean to the sound. Ocean beaches and rain forests highlight opportunities along the coast.

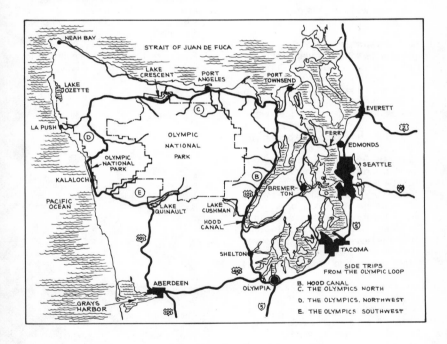

Mt. Ellinor, left, and Mt. Washington from Lake Cushman   **17**

B   HOOD CANAL

Oysters, rhododendrons, waterfalls, and spectacular high views from the saltwater of Hood Canal to the foothills of the Olympics. Off Highway 101, Quilcene to Hoodsport.

CAMPGROUNDS

Potlatch State Park — 34 sites including 18 trailer units in an open, undefined area on Hood Canal. A popular year-round camp. Oysters and clams at low tide. Restrooms. Piped water. Fee. 3 miles south of Hoodsport.

Lake Cushman State Park — 80 campsites with 31 trailer hookups in an irregular wooded development. Sites in timber and undergrowth away from the lake. Boat launching. Reservoir-type lake full of stumps at low water. Restrooms. Piped water. Fee. 7 miles west of Hoodsport. Campground beyond the boat-picnic area at the first park sign.

Staircase — 63 campsites on pleasant well-organized big-timber loops on the Skokomish River in Olympic National Park. Restrooms. Piped water. 19 miles west of Hoodsport.

Hamma Hamma — 12 sites in a wooded flat near the Hamma Hamma River. Some next to the river. Others on wooded loops. Pit toilets. Well water. Fee. 7 miles west of Eldon.

Lena Creek — 14 sites. Most near the Hamma Hamma River in pleasant vine maple grove. Pit toilets. Well water. 9 miles west of Eldon.

Collins — 14 sites in wooded, river-bottom area on Duckabush River. Pit toilets. Well water. 5 miles west of Highway 101 on road No. 2515.

Dosewallips State Park — 153 sites, 40 with trailer hookups in very popular area on Hood Canal. Most sites in open, unshaded loops. A few near the river. Oysters and clams. Restrooms. Piped water. Fee. 24 miles north of Hoodsport.

Steelhead — An undeveloped camping area. No facilities. Along the Dosewallips River. 9.5 miles west of Brinnon.

Elkhorn — 18 sites in a very pleasant timbered area on the Dosewallips River. Many sites on the river. Pit toilets. Piped water. 11 miles west of Brinnon.

Dosewallips — 33 sites in open big-timber area. Sites along the river and on wooded loops. A peaceful campground. But not recommended for trailers, entry road is too steep. Restrooms. Piped water. 15 miles west of Brinnon.

Seal Rock — 35 sites. All on wooded loops away from the water. 10 picnic sites along Hood Canal. Only Forest Service campground in the nation with oyster-picking opportunities. Restroom. Piped water. 2 miles north of Brinnon. Fee. Trailer limit, 22 feet.

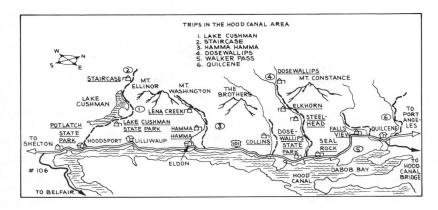

TRIPS IN THE HOOD CANAL AREA
1. LAKE CUSHMAN
2. STAIRCASE
3. HAMMA HAMMA
4. DOSEWALLIPS
5. WALKER PASS
6. QUILCENE

Rainbow—9 picnic sites in wooded tract just off Highway 101 near road to Mt. Walker. Pit toilets. Piped water. 5 miles south of Quilcene. Fee.

Falls View — 20 tent and 15 trailer sites in rhododendron forest just off Highway 101. Restrooms. Piped water. 4 miles south of Quilcene.

Mt. Rainier in moonlight and Puget Sound country from Big Creek Road

B HOOD CANAL

1 LAKE CUSHMAN

BIG CREEK VIEWS

Puget Sound and Hood Canal against a backdrop — on a clear day — of Rainier, Adams, and St. Helens. With the lights of Tacoma at night.

Early morning or late evening for the clearest views. With a road map pick out Carr Inlet and North Bay, Nisqually Flats, too, if it is very clear.

Drive west from the center of Hoodsport on the Lake Cushman road, turning right at a T intersection about 8 miles from Hoodsport, 2 miles beyond Lake Cushman State Park. In another 1.5 miles turn sharply west onto Big Creek road No. 2419. Viewpoint in 6 miles. Another .8 mile for a pretty waterfall off Mt. Washington.

The final spur is well-graded but a cliffhanger and steep in spots.

MT. ELLINOR TRAIL

Hike 1 mile or 2 through pleasant forest to increasingly sweeping views of Mt. Adams past Mt. Rainier to Seattle.

In the first mile, watch for viewpoints through the trees from a ridge-edge to the left of the trail. Look down here onto Lake Cushman.

In another mile — the way gets steeper now — trail reaches a small subalpine basin just below the peak. Look for outlook spots atop huge boulders to the right. Lunch here with Adams, Rainier and Seattle.

Find trail off Big Creek road No. 2419 (see above) at 5 miles.

MT. ROSE TRAIL

It's almost 5 miles to the summit. But a mile hike uphill leads to startling views of the Olympics out over Lake Cushman.

From the T intersection (see above) turn left on road No. 24. Trailhead on the right in about 3 miles.

Trail starts out in timber but breaks out into views in the first mile. Best views of course from the top of the mountain.

HOOD CANAL HATCHERY

The only freshwater-saltwater hatchery operated by the State Department of Fisheries.

Between the highway and Hood Canal at Hoodsport. Salmon return to collecting

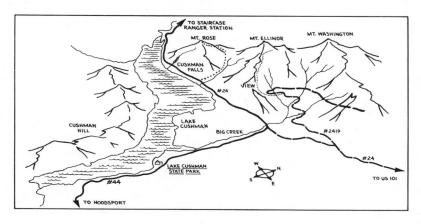

Lake Cushman from Mt. Ellinor Trail

pens each fall to spawn. Several hundred may be seen at one time trying to reach artificial stream pens where they were hatched.

CUSHMAN FALLS

A car-window view of a 70-foot falls off Mt. Rose into Lake Cushman. Drive 11 miles from Hoodsport toward Staircase Campground in Olympic National Park.

Falls north of the road near the end of the lake.

Skokomish River valley from forest road No. 2451 above Staircase

2 STAIRCASE

STAIRCASE TRAIL

First a staircase of rapids and then an easy hike past moss-draped groves of maples and alders.

Cross the bridge over the North Fork of the Skokomish at the upper end of the campground, finding the trail to the right of the ranger's house.

Pass the noisy, scenic Staircase Rapids in less than a half-mile. Loiter here for certain, catching new glimpses from every stream-side boulder.

Continue on the trail along the river through several soft-lighted, rain forest-like flats for about 2 miles before crossing the river by bridge and looping back to camp on an old road. If the river is low, take time to explore the low flats below the trail. Elk winter here and give the area its park-like quality.

Camp spots and picnic places before the trail crosses north across the river.

SHADY LANE TRAIL

Just what it's named. A pleasant .75-mile stroll along the west side of the river from the ranger's house, left to the park boundary.

Cross the bridge, finding the trail in front of the ranger's house. Part of the trail near the river was blasted from rock. The old Staircase Trail, now grown over and abandoned, climbed over the top of the bluff. Return the same way. 🚶

DRY CREEK TRAIL

A relatively level trail along Lake Cushman with views out over the lake at surrounding peaks.

Find the trailhead on the left beyond the causeway bridge at the northwest end of Lake Cushman. (Trail to the right connects with the Shady Lane Trail in the park.)

The path follows the lake for about 1.1 miles before heading uphill along Dry Creek into Dry Creek Canyon in another .6 mile.

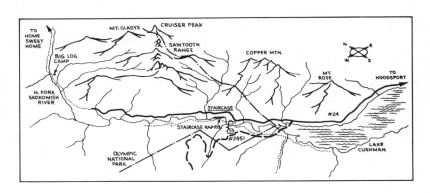

B HOOD CANAL

3 HAMMA HAMMA

HIGH VIEW DRIVE

In June, bear grass and rhododendrons framed against the deep blue of Hood Canal. Views too of the Kitsap Peninsula, the Cascades, Baker, and Rainier. And some days even more.

Turn west off Highway 101 onto the Hamma Hamma River road No. 25 about 2 miles north of Eldon, taking the first logging road north at 2.4 miles.

For the first 5 miles, the road No. 2510 climbs along a ridge top in timber with only occasional views both east and west. But shortly after crossing into Olympic National Forest at about 6 miles, the road jumps out for open views, creeping along the side of a mountain for 2 miles before ducking back into a valley and dropping down to the river, and the crossing again. ⟞

CABIN CREEK ROAD

Mt. Bretherton, Jefferson Ridge, and Cruiser Peak in one of the few views of the Olympic peaks from the Hood Canal area.

Drive north on the Cabin Creek road No. 2402 — the first logging road to the right beyond Hamma Hamma Campground. Drive about 1.3 miles to the end of the second switchback for views up the Hamma Hamma valley and the peaks. No higher views as the road continues up Cabin Creek. Turn around at the viewpoint. ⟞

LENA LAKES

Hike a little less than 3 miles on an easy grade to one of the most popular lakes in this part of the Olympics. More than 10,000 hikers a year. Now closed to trail bikes.

Follow road No. 25 (turn west off Highway 101 about 1.5 miles north of Eldon) to a well-marked trail junction near Lena Creek Campground.

From the lake, hike either 4 miles to Upper Lena Lake or only 1 mile up the Brothers Trail (to the right at the upper end of Lena Lake) to the quiet Valley of Silent Man.

PUTVIN TRAIL

Hike to alpine meadows with views up at Mt. Stone and Mt. Skokomish and into the Boulder Creek Basin.

Find the trail from the end of the Hamma Hamma road No. 25 off spur road No. 2466 in a mile. (The spur road was closed a half-mile from the trailhead in 1982.)

The maintained trail ends in less than a mile, but way trails head to meadows with views in another .7 mile.

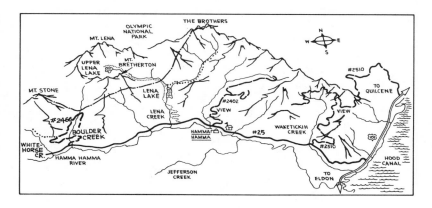

24

Camping at Lower Lena Lake

B HOOD CANAL

4 DOSEWALLIPS

DOSEWALLIPS FALLS

A tumbling series of steep cascades through a narrow canyon beside a steep road to the Dosewallips Campground in Olympic National Park.

Near the end of the Dosewallips road, 15 miles west of Highway 101. Turn west just north of Dosewallips State Park.

Best view of the falls from the road at the bottom. Views down on the cascades from boulders near the road at the top. Hike back, too, from the campground, less than a half-mile.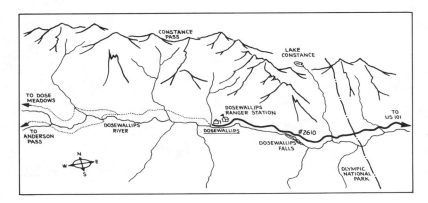

Note also the rounded, pillow-like rocks in the cliffs near the falls. They were formed when molten lava flowed and cooled under an ancient sea. Rockhounds can also see colorful limestone breccias and weirdly beautiful mineralization from the contact of hot rock with cold and other violent geologic processes.

DOSE FORKS TRAIL

A forested trail leads through virgin timber and patches of rhododendron to a river crossing in a rich forest setting. 1.5 miles.

Trail leaves the far end of the Dosewallips Campground beyond the ranger complex, climbing above the river and making its way through rich forest before dropping down to the river, and the crossing again.

Either continue on the trail across the river or explore the grove of huge trees at the crossing. The series of shelters along this trail have been removed. Camp spots remain.

MT. JUPITER RIDGE

Fantastic springtime rhododendron walk with bonus views of Mt. Rainier, Adams, the Brothers and Jupiter too.

Trail switchbacks about 8 times up through rhododendron groves to the side of a ridge and then sweeps along less steeply toward the base of Jupiter. Summit in 7 miles. Walk as far as you want.

Best views, though, of Rainier and Adams as you walk back.

To find the unmarked road, drive 2.6 miles south from the Dosewallips State Park on Highway 101, turning west about 100 yards beyond the "Black Point" sign on an unmarked road No. 2620.

Follow the narrow, one-track road, which ranges from terrible to fair (it's all outside the national forest) about 6.7 miles to a small parking area and trail sign at the end of spur No. 011.

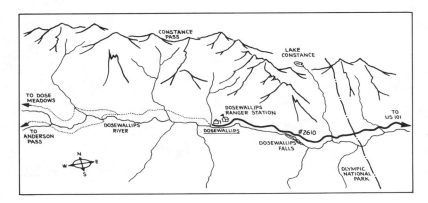

B HOOD CANAL

5 WALKER PASS

MT. WALKER

Popular twin vistas from picnic areas at 3000 feet just 5 miles by well-developed gravel road from Highway 101.

Drive 5 miles south of Quilcene. Watch for signs on the east side of the road at Walker Pass.

From the south viewpoint — first on the road — see Mt. Rainier, Seattle (the Space Needle), Tacoma, Everett, the Cascades, and the Hood Canal Floating Bridge.

From the north viewpoint add Jupiter, Constance, and Buckhorn Mountains in the Olympics, the Big Quilcene River canyon, Mt. Baker, Quilcene Bay, and Hood Canal. Road closed from October 1 to May 1.

Rhododendrons from May to July. ▰

RAINBOW CANYON

A short walk down a pleasant trail to a bench about 40 feet above the Big Quilcene River.

Watch for trail sign to the far side of the Rainbow picnic area. A 10- to 15-minute walk to the bench. Watch for a small waterfall to the left near the end of the trail. Fisherman's path leads off to the right, dropping down to the river with a steep scramble the last 20 feet or so.

CAMPGROUND FALLS

A wispy little falls that drops like a delicate veil 100 feet into the Big Quilcene River. Flows its best during the high-water periods of spring and fall. Sometimes disappears entirely in dry spells.

Find trail at the south end of the Falls View Campground. Trail to the west leads to a fenced viewpoint, looping back to the parking area.

Rhododendrons, twin flowers, and tiger lilies in mid-June.

STATE SHELLFISH LABORATORY

Not keyed to public use. But visitors can sometimes find aquarium displays in tanks behind facility buildings. Oysters and small-neck clams can be taken from public beaches near the lab. However, visitors must not disturb shellfish in the iron baskets on the beach. They contain tests. The lagoon behind the beach is also closed.

Drive north on Highway 101 about 2.25 miles beyond the Seal Rock Campground, turning east at signs indicating Camp Parsons of the Boy Scouts. Follow the road to end.

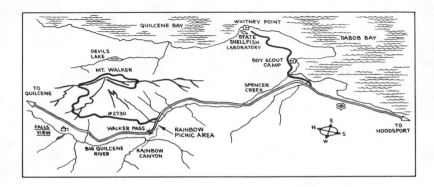

Rhododendrons and Mt. Constance from Mt. Walker

B HOOD CANAL

6 QUILCENE

MT. ZION
On a clear day you can almost see forever. From Vancouver, B.C., south to Adams. With Port Angeles, Victoria, the Space Needle, all the Cascades, Baker, Glacier, and Rainier, the Strait of Juan de Fuca, Hood Canal, and Puget Sound — and everything in between.

About 1.75 miles by trail.

Drive north out of Quilcene on Highway 101 for 2 miles, taking the first major side road to the left. At Lords Lake take road No. 2909 to Bon Jon Pass. At Bon Jon Pass turn right for 2 miles, watching for trail sign on the right side of the road. Return by the same road. Lookout has been burned.

Trail climbs persistently through timber to the lookout site at 4273 feet. Rhododendrons bloom most of the way in June and July.

NATIONAL FISH HATCHERY
Rare albino trout in a formal hatchery display open the year-round. Silver salmon are trapped at the federal hatchery during heavy runs during late September and November.

Formal displays of fish in tanks are explained in tape-recorded lectures. The hatchery, operated by the United States Fish and Wildlife Service, raises about 650,000 silver, 2 million chinook, and 5 million chum salmon each year.

Drive south from Quilcene on Highway 101. Watch for sign in about 2 miles. Turn west.

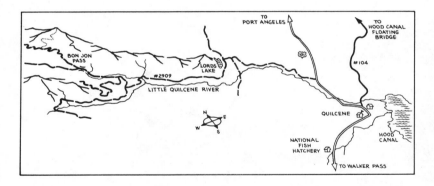

Hood Canal Floating Bridge

C THE OLYMPICS, NORTH

Lush forest trails, waterfalls, crystal lakes, spectacular alpine flower meadows, and sweeping lookout views — all just off Highway 101 between Blyn and Forks on the Olympic Peninsula.

CAMPGROUNDS

Sequim Bay State Park — 86 sites with 26 hookups in a heavily used wooded area on a bluff above the bay. Boat launching. Clams. 4 miles southeast of Sequim. Restrooms. Piped water. Fee.

Dungeness Forks — 9 sites in a pleasant wooded area in the fork of

Lake Crescent

the Dungeness and Gray Wolf Rivers. 13 miles south of Sequim. Pit toilets. Well water. Road not recommended for trailers.

Slab — 3 sites in a relatively primitive development. 17 miles southwest of Sequim. Pit toilets.

Deer Park — 10 sites and 2 shelters in a beautiful alpine timber setting surrounded by meadows at 5400. Not suitable for trailers. 17 miles from Highway 101 over narrow mountain road. Pit toilets. Piped water from spring.

Heart O' the Hills — 105 sites on a series of forest loops. A pleasant area. Sites well separated. 5.4 miles from Port Angeles. Restrooms. Piped water. Campfire programs. Fee.

Elwha — 41 sites in an open area under moss-covered maples. Open in winter. 3 miles from Highway 101 on Elwha River road. Restrooms. Piped water. Campfire programs. Fee.

Altaire — 29 sites, all blanketed by the sound of the Elwha River. Some sites near the river but most on forest loops under moss-tinted forest canopy. 4 miles from highway on Elwha River road. Restrooms. Piped water. Fee.

Boulder Creek — 50 sites on high timbered bench. Older sites to the right of the entrance road. Newer sites to the left. 12 miles up the Elwha River road. Restrooms. Piped water. Small trailers only. Fee.

Fairholm — 87 sites at the west end of Lake Crescent. Some walk-in sites along the lake. Most on wooded loops. Restrooms. Piped water. Campfire program. Fee.

Soleduck — 84 sites in two campgrounds. The older site, first on the road, in heavily thinned timber. The newer campground in a more natural timber setting. 12 miles on the Soleduck River road. Restrooms. Piped water. Campfire programs. Fee. Hot spring resort nearby open year around.

Klahowya — 33 tent and 12 trailer sites in wooded setting along the Soleduck River. A pleasant campground. 8 miles from Sappho. Pit toilets. Piped water. Pioneer nature trail. Fee.

Dungeness Recreation Area — 60 sites on bluff overlooking Dungeness Spit. Restrooms. Piped water. Fee.

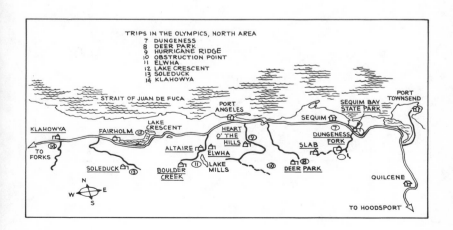

TRIPS IN THE OLYMPICS, NORTH AREA
7 DUNGENESS
8 DEER PARK
9 HURRICANE RIDGE
10 OBSTRUCTION POINT
11 ELWHA
12 LAKE CRESCENT
13 SOLEDUCK
14 KLAHOWYA

C THE OLYMPICS, NORTH

7 DUNGENESS

High roads lead to views of the Dungeness and Gray Wolf River valleys.
Turn south off Highway 101 just west of Sequim Bay State Park on forest road No. 2909. Watch for fork in road about 1 mile beyond the Louella Forest Service Work Camp.
Fork left leads to Dungeness views in 8 miles. Keep right onto road No. 2950 about 1 mile beyond the fork. Best views toward wooded Townsend and Buckhorn from Three O'Clock Ridge at the 3000-foot level a little more than halfway.
For Gray Wolf views turn right at the fork on No. 2958, driving past the Dungeness Forks Campground, taking the first road, No. 2927, uphill to the west about 1 mile beyond the campground. Follow No. 2927 over the ridge, turning left onto road No. 2926, marked Slab Camp. Views over the Gray Wolf valley beyond Slab Camp.

DUNGENESS SPIT
You can look down on this entire spit from bluffs and roads along the shore, but to truly savor the sudden wildness of this national refuge for sea and shore birds, you must walk its shores or climb its piles of driftwood.
From the center of Sequim on Highway 101 turn north toward Dungeness and then west toward the old schoolhouse and the Dungeness River. Follow main roads now as they wander westward sometimes on bluffs, overlooking the spit, and sometimes through pleasant farm country to the Dungeness Recreation Area.
Find the beach trails off a parking lot beyond the campground.
To reach the beach, follow the main trail down the bluff and then wander where you will. No formal trails on the spit at all. Walk out on one side and return on the other.
It's about 7 miles to the lighthouse. Or just hike out to Graveyard Spit, about halfway, exploring where you will. Lots of migrating birds in the winter. Shellfish on the beaches. Solitude if you're willing to walk a mile or two.

Nearest camping
Dungeness Recreation Area

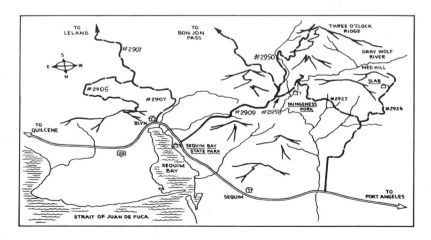

Dungeness Spit

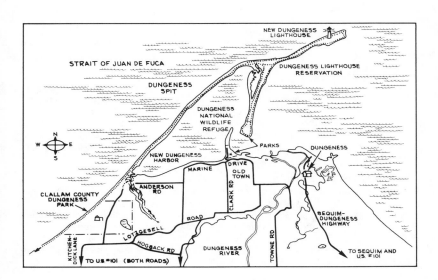

Deer at Deer Park

8   DEER PARK

Alpine flower slopes, grazed by deer and topped by a viewpoint. Highest camping area in Olympic National Park. 17 miles south of Highway 101. Watch for green sign on the south side of the highway about 3 miles east of Port Angeles.

BLUE MOUNTAIN VIEW

Drive if you must, but better yet, walk the mile along the road or across the open alpine meadows. Views of Port Angeles, the Strait of Juan de Fuca, Vancouver Island, the San Juan Islands, Baker, Gray Wolf Ridge, The Needles, and Cameron Glaciers.

Road climbs above the Deer Park Campground to just below a former lookout site at 6007. Magnificent sunsets fill the deep valleys with changing shades of red and purple. Walk up after dark to see glow of lowland lights and a sky bursting with stars. 🚶

OBSTRUCTION POINT TRAIL

A hike of less than a mile leads to the open slopes of Green Mountain with views over the Grand Creek valley with glimpses of Grand and Moose Lakes.

Walk the abandoned road downhill past the ranger station, ending in about 1 mile. Trail climbs through decreasing alpine timber to sweeping flower meadows at nearly 6000.

Trail continues on to Obstruction Point, 7.6 miles. Steep snowfields pose a hazard along the trail through midsummer most years. 🚶

SLAB CAMP TRAIL

A 1-mile hike along the ridge east of the Deer Park Campground leads to changing views of the valley.

Trail leaves the campground to the right of the first campsite. Trail to Three Forks Shelter turns downhill in .25 mile. Keep left along the ridge. At about 1 mile the trail drops slowly downhill to the park boundary and Slab Camp in 5 miles.

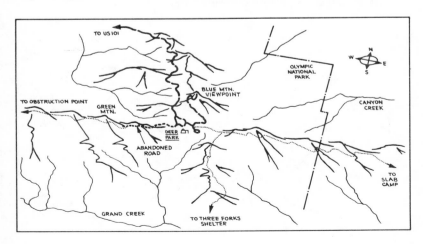

C THE OLYMPICS, NORTH

9 HURRICANE RIDGE

Most popular and heavily used of the alpine areas in Olympic National Park. Formal nature trails afford easy access to flower meadows and vistas of the snowcapped central Olympic peaks and the Strait of Juan de Fuca.

Turn south off Highway 101 in Port Angeles. Watch for park headquarters sign. 18 miles to Hurricane Ridge Lodge. Another 1.25 miles to picnic area. No camping.

LAKE CREEK TRAIL

A level trail wanders 2 miles through mossy, old-growth timber to a ranch at the edge of the park. No lake. An extremely pleasant place for an evening stroll.

Trail leaves the far end of the Heart O' the Hills Campground off E loop. Watch for sign.

MEADOW TRAIL

Stroll across sprawling flower meadows to possible views of mountain goats and certain views of the main Olympic peaks and the Strait of Juan de Fuca.

From the Hurricane Ridge Lodge follow trail signs uphill toward Heather Park-Lake Angeles-Heart O' the Hills returning to the highway at about 4.6 miles down the switchbacks of the 1.2-mile Switchback Trail.

The way climbs upward at first but then follows the ridge across flower meadow after flower meadow with views both north and south. If you have time take one of the spur trails to other unmarked vistas. 🚶

HURRICANE HILL

A paved nature trail leads 1.4 miles to a .3-mile trail loop with marked vista points looking both north and south.

Drive 1.3 miles beyond the lodge. Trail follows an abandoned roadway along a ridge to the top of the hill.

Vista signs identify park peaks sweeping east from Blue Mountain, past Seattle, Olympus to Boulder. Sign on the north side of the ridge identifies features on the Strait.

A pleasant walk even on rainy days. The flowers alone are worth the trip. 🚶

CIRQUE, MEADOW, AND HIGH RIDGE LOOPS

Three small loop trails, .25- to .5-mile long, or a connected loop of about 1 mile circle meadows and ridges above Hurricane Ridge Lodge.

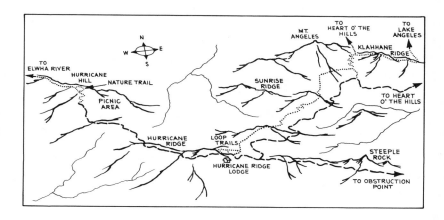

Avalanche lilies on Klahhane Ridge Trail

Signs identify the loops at trailheads near the highway, across from the lodge.

Strictly — of necessity — a highly controlled area where visitors are implored to walk only on paved trails. Random heavy foot traffic quickly destroys plant life in such high alpine sites.

Trails lead to ridges with views toward Port Angeles and the Strait, affording continuous views of the central Olympic peaks. Deer, marmots, chipmunks, hawks, and jays. 🚶

C THE OLYMPICS, NORTH

10 OBSTRUCTION POINT

A narrow dirt road winds 8.4 miles through alpine timber and across open slopes above the Lillian River to the snow-patched alpine flower fields of Obstruction Point.

Take the gravel road south just east of the Hurricane Ridge Lodge. Trailers prohibited.

GRAND LAKE TRAIL

Through fields of flowers, past snow-fed tarns to crystal views of Olympic peaks. With marmots, deer, and hawks along the way.

From the parking area at the end of the road walk south along the ridge. Gentle snowfields in the first 1000 feet. Rock cairns mark the route.

Two clear snow-fed pools across the meadows to the east of the trail just before it ducks around the right side of the first small peak.

Best view of Olympus in 2 miles, as the trail drops quickly to the lake. 🔥

DEER PARK TRAIL

A thin line etched on the side of a mountain leads to high views of the Grand Creek valley. Listen for the whistle of marmots on the slopes below.

Hike east out of the parking area, taking the trail left across the steep slopes of the ridge between Obstruction Peak and Elk Mountain. Steep snowfields may block the way. Trail continues to Deer Park, 7.6 miles. Walk as far as you wish or as snowfields allow. Don't attempt to cross steep snow without proper climbing gear. 🔥

OBSTRUCTION PEAK

No marked trail but a short climb from the parking area leads to higher views (6450) of all the surrounding country, including Mt. Angeles and the Morse Creek valley to the north and the Strait.

Follow established paths when possible. That plants can live at all in such thin-soil, barren slopes is a miracle of sorts. A single scuff of a foot can destroy a century of growth. 🔥

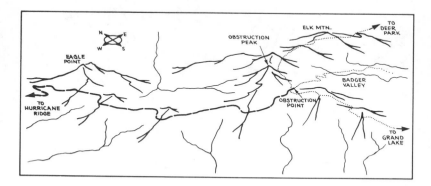

Hurricane Ridge Lodge and Mt. Carrie

C   THE OLYMPICS, NORTH

11   ELWHA

WEST ELWHA TRAIL
Elk in the winter graze on grass meadows under moss-laden trees.

Trail leaves the upper end of the Altaire Campground, away from the river near bulletin board display. A short walk leads into green-lit forest tunnels of moss-covered maple. Trail leads 2.6 miles to the park boundary. Trail climbs away from the river most of the time, touching it only occasionally.

Other trails skirt the edge of the campground, leading down short spurs into the forest. 🚶

GOAT VIEWS
Binocular views of mountain goats along the rock ridges west of the road between the park boundary and the Elwha Campground. Goats can be seen all times of the year. The park, however, is considering removing them.

LAKE MILLS TRAIL
A pleasant, level 1.9-mile trail along the west side of Lake Mills with several intimate beaches along the way.

Turn south off the road to Boulder Creek Campground just beyond the powerhouse complex at the end of Lake Mills. The road looks like a driveway but actually goes past the house near the junction.

The trail — signed as Boulder Creek Trail — starts uphill just before the spur road ends in a parking lot and boat-launch area on the lake. The trail alternately winds through big timber overlooking the lake and drops down the small sandy sections of beach. Ends at Boulder Creek. 🚶

LOWER BOULDER CREEK FALLS
Cascades of white over rich green moss in a bower of towering trees.

An easy 1.5 miles through timber from the Boulder Creek Campground on the Appleton Pass Trail. The trail leaves the upper, west, end of the campground. Keep left at junction with Boulder Lake Trail in about 1 mile. Sign indicates falls shortly after trail crosses the north fork of Boulder Creek. 🚶

OLYMPIC HOT SPRINGS
Hike downhill a few hundred yards from the Boulder Creek Campground. These springs, only a few decades ago, heated a formal pool at a formal resort. All of the resort buildings were destroyed. The hot spring pools you find there now were man-made by bathers who have refused to let the springs return to any sort of normal state. Expect little and you won't be disappointed.

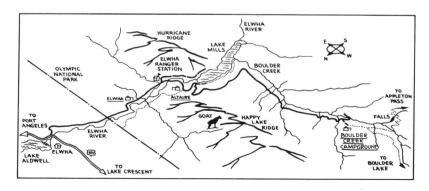

Elwha River

12   LAKE CRESCENT

MARYMERE FALLS
A formal nature trail leads through rich forest to a slender, shaded 90-foot falls.

Find trail off the parking lot beside the Storm King Information Center on Lake Crescent. 1.5 miles around the trail. Guide booklet available at the trailhead explains the ecology of the forest community, describing displays along the way. 🚶

LAKE SUTHERLAND VIEWS
High logging roads outside the park lead to views over Lake Sutherland and the Strait of Juan de Fuca.

Turn south off Highway 101 onto the South Shore road just east of Lake Sutherland. In less than a half-mile turn uphill off the shore road onto a forest road.

Keep uphill at all intersections, turning sharply left at the first and bearing right at the second. Road No. 3050 climbs along side of Baldy Ridge for views. 🚗

PYRAMID PEAK TRAIL
A steady climb part way to an old aircraft-spotter's station leads to vistas over crystal-blue Lake Crescent.

Drive 3.5 miles past the Fairholm Campground on the North Shore Lake Crescent road, watching for the trail sign on the left.

The trail starts in timber as it traverses the mountain to the east, breaking out for open views between 1 and 2 miles. It's 3.5 miles to the top. 🚶

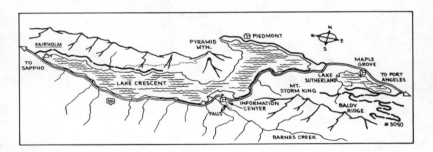

C THE OLYMPICS, NORTH

13 SOLEDUCK

SALMON CASCADE

A small waterfall explodes with the violence of salmon hurling themselves against the torrent and into rocks in an effort to spawn in the upper reaches of the Soleduck River.

Watch for a sign and parking area on the west side of the road to Soleduck Hot Springs, 4 miles from Highway 101. 🚗

A short path leads to rock ledges overlooking the cascades and leaping fish. Big pools below the cascades. Best display in September and October.

SOLEDUCK FALLS

Actually a fistful of small falls. Three to four separate fingers of water tumble into a narrow gorge through clefts eroded in rock.

1 mile by trail from the parking area at the end of the Soleduck road, 1.4 miles beyond the campground. Take trail fork to the right in front of the shelter to reach the

Salmon leaping Soleduck River cascades

Soleduck Hot Springs

falls and a bridge. Best views are across the bridge.

The shelter — for 10 — provides a good place to picnic but no place to camp. Extremely heavy visitor-use prohibits anything resembling privacy. 🏃🚶

LOVER'S LANE TRAIL

Certainly a pleasant place for lovers. But worth a visit too by the temporarily uninvolved.

An easy, water-grade trail travels within earshot of the Soleduck River, weaving into timber and then back to mossy, open places beside the river.

Take the trail back to the resort area from Soleduck Falls after crossing the bridge (see above). 3.7-mile trip from the road end to the resort. Or walk out from the resort and return.

To find trail at the hot spring resort, walk past the lodge on the right, finding the trail beyond the swimming pool beside a cabin on the uphill side. Sign just beyond the cabin. 🚶

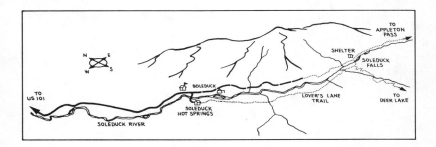

14   KLAHOWYA

Two forest roads outside Olympic National Park lead to spectacular views of the Olympics, the Pacific, and the Strait of Juan de Fuca.

NORTH POINT (KLOSHE NANICH)
In the evening, startling sunsets over the ocean. And during the day, sweeping vistas that include the Strait, Olympus, Tom, La Push, and even James Island.

Take the first road north off Highway 101 just west of the Klahowya Campground. Road leads to the Snider Forest Service Work Center.

Find forest road No. 3041 in the middle of the complex. The road climbs west at the start and then switches back to the east. The lookout, in 8 miles. 3340 feet. Other vista points along the way. 🚐

HYAS VIEWPOINT
The best view of Olympus, highest peak on the peninsula, from a road. With Forks and the Pacific at an arm's length to the west.

Turn south off Highway 101 onto forest road No. 29 just across from the entrance to the Klahowya Campground, bearing right in about .5 mile on road No. 2923. Continue on No. 2923, watching for lookout spur road at about 12 miles from highway. Lookout tower has been removed.

To continue on to Forks without returning to Klahowya follow No. 2923 southerly until it joins road No. 29 on the South Fork of the Sitkum River. Forks is 18 miles from the lookout. 🚐

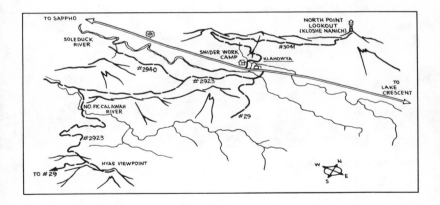

Soleduck valley from North Point Lookout   **49**

North end of Rialto Beach

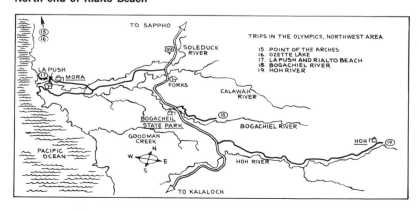

TO SAPPHO

SOLEDUCK RIVER

TRIPS IN THE OLYMPICS, NORTHWEST AREA

15. POINT OF THE ARCHES
16. OZETTE LAKE
17. LA PUSH AND RIALTO BEACH
18. BOGACHIEL RIVER
19. HOH RIVER

LA PUSH
MORA

FORKS

CALAWAH RIVER

BOGACHIEL STATE PARK

BOGACHIEL RIVER

GOODMAN CREEK

PACIFIC OCEAN

N
W   E
S

HOH

HOH RIVER

TO KALALOCH

D THE OLYMPICS, NORTHWEST

From glistening summer beaches to dim-lit winter rain forests; from delicate blue Japanese fishing floats to lush green forest fern; from eagles to elk.

Those are only a small part of the offerings of heavily used western side of the Olympic Peninsula. Drive south and west from Forks, north from Aberdeen-Hoquiam, or south from Neah Bay.

CAMPGROUNDS

Mora — 91 sites on deeply shaded forest loops. Closest park campground to the Rialto and La Push beach areas. 11.9 miles from Highway 101. Turn west 2 miles north of Forks. Restrooms. Piped water. Campfire programs. Some facilities open in winter. Fee.

Bogachiel State Park — 41 sites on wooded loops near the Bogachiel River. Less crowded than most state parks. 6 miles south of Forks on Highway 101. Restrooms. Piped water. Fee.

Hoh — 95 sites on quiet loops in rain forest. 19 miles from Highway 101. Turn east 14 miles south of Forks. Restrooms. Piped water. Campfire programs. Fee.

La Push — Camping is permitted by some resorts in La Push. Some offer sites near the beach. Inquire locally for rates. Facilities vary.

15   POINT OF THE ARCHES

A wild corner of ocean splendors here. Sea stacks by the dozen. Sweeping sandy beaches. Tidepools. Even shipwrecks. But only for those willing to walk.

To reach this corner of Olympic National Park follow roads southwesterly from Neah Bay. (Be certain to visit the Indian museum there.)

After crossing the Waatch River follow beach roads around Mukkaw Bay to a parking area shortly after the shore road starts uphill. And remember: This is on the Makah Indian Reservation and you are guests on this land.

SHI SHI BEACH

One long, sweeping sand beach between two rugged and scenic headlands.

From the parking area south of Mukkaw Bay walk about 1.5 miles to the park boundary. Find a downhill trail. Camp spots here, with water, or in dozens of other places, without water, down the beach to the south.

From this point, walk north along the beach through rocks at low tide to see parts of a wrecked ship — some on shore and some in the water. Tidepools, rock spires and small coves along the way.

A sand beach stretches south another 1.5 miles to Petroleum Creek — and beyond.

POINT OF THE ARCHES

One of the most dramatic collections of sea stacks, tidepools and hidden coves along the entire Northwest coast.

From the parking area south of Mukkaw Bay hike to the park boundary. Either drop to the beach here or follow the old, overgrown and often muddy road to Petroleum Creek. From Petroleum Creek to the Arches, about 1 mile. (You'll find some fairly artful shacks hidden in the trees. Although privately built, none are privately owned.)

Best exploring here at low tide. Carry a guide book to help you identify all of the sea creatures. And if you pick them up, put them back. Nature, even here, has its limits.

PORTAGE HEAD

A grand vista of the coast and headlands here from a long-abandoned coast artillery observation bunker.

The trailhead is unmarked and hard to find. From the park boundary, walk back north along the road to Mukkaw Bay about 1 mile finding an unmaintained path through the brush that leads gradually uphill around a hillside and then finally to the top of the head.

The view here seems never ending. Look south to the Point of the Arches, north to Tatoosh Island and Cape Flattery and straight down into a rage of rocks and tidepools.

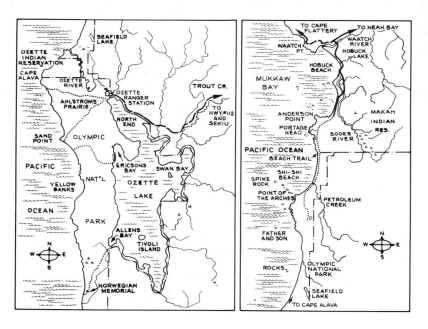

Shi Shi Beach

16 OZETTE LAKE

Trails to the Pacific Ocean here exceed the 2-mile limit usually fixed for this book. But they are so flat and so popular they cannot be ignored.

To reach the trailhead at the north end of Ozette Lake, turn south off Highway 112 to Neah Bay just west of Sekiu, driving to the end of the road.

CAPE ALAVA

Hike across a prairie and through rich forest to the westernmost point in the "lower" U.S.

At a trail fork just across the Ozette River, hike right on a path that crosses Ahlstrom's Prairie — an old farm site — and then continues through forest to the ocean in a total of 3.3 miles.

Hike north along the beach to Cannon Ball Island with its tumble of round concretions just below a cliff. The archeological site at an old buried Indian village has been closed.

SAND POINT

A small rock pinnacle marks the north end of a beautiful beach that sweeps south to a headland at Yellow Banks.

Turn south at the trail junction across the Ozette River, crossing soggy meadows on a puncheon path to reach the beach in about 3 miles.

Find tide pools in offshore rocks near Yellow Banks to the south in about 1.5 miles. Explore steeper and narrower beaches north of the point.

BEACH LOOP

Hike to Cape Alava and then south along the beach to Sand Point before returning to Lake Ozette. A 9-mile loop.

A full day's walk. Schedule your trip so that you can walk the beaches at low tide.

Watch for Indian carvings on rocks at a small headland halfway down the beach.

"Hole in the Wall" near Rialto Beach

17   LA PUSH AND RIALTO BEACH

Sand and rock-pool ocean beaches on both sides of the Quillayute River and the Quillayute Indian village of La Push.

Turn west off Highway 101 about 2 miles north of Forks. 11 miles to Rialto Beach; 14.2 miles to La Push.

HOLE IN THE WALL

A natural rock bridge still being carved by the sea. Walk through at low tide.

From the Rialto Beach Picnic Area hike north along the beach to Ellen Creek, 1 mile. Wade or cross the creek on logs. Easiest at low tide. Find the tunneled rock north of the creek. Views through it back toward La Push.

Watch for rusted debris of wrecked ships in the low-tide rocks along the beach.

JAMES POND

A short, loop trail across the road from the Mora Campground Ranger Station leads to the quiet environment of a rain forest swamp. Frogs, ducks and heron in their own private lair. A must walk if you stay in the campground.

FIRST BEACH

Although one of the most accessible beaches, it still gets light public use. A broad beach from the lighthouse in La Push south to the first headland. Indian reservation land.

Drive to La Push, parking on road spur near edge of town.

SECOND BEACH

A sandy, sweeping beach with towering sea stacks offshore. Closed by sea-etched rock headlands at either end.

Walk a .6-mile trail south of the road at the eastern edge of La Push. Watch for parking area sign. Trail starts on Indian reservation land.

THIRD BEACH

A curving mile-long sand beach enclosed on the north by Teahwhit Head and on the south by Taylor Point with its waterfall plunging directly into the sea.

Find the half-mile trail about 1.5 miles east of La Push. Parking strip on the south side of the road.

Some people camp on the beach. But heavy public use makes privacy impossible.

Wilderness beach trail to the Hoh leaves far end of the beach. Watch for target signs.

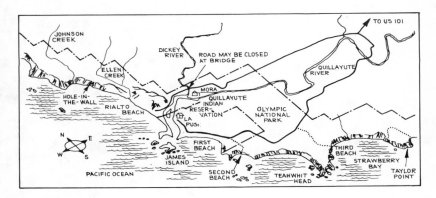

18   BOGACHIEL RIVER

Walk here and remember!

Timber companies before have sought to claim the timber of this valley for their pulp mills and saws. And almost certainly they will try to do so again.

So when you hike up this valley for only 2 miles decide whether this magnificent example of "old and decaying trees...doddering to the ground" ought to be "conserved" with an ax, as the timber companies have argued in the past. Or preserved, as conservation groups have always insisted, as part of the Olympic National Park.

Decide as you walk whether the soft beauty of the vine maples, spruce, fir and hemlock — centuries old and mantled with moss over carpets of fern — can be equated with mountains of pulp chips piled by a paper mill.

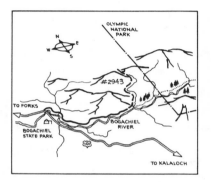

And make certain note of what you decide. For what you recall on some tomorrow may be all that will save these forests again.

Turn east from Highway 101 onto an unmarked gravel road just north of the Bogachiel River and Bogachiel State Park. Follow a new logging road about 4 miles, turning off on a rough, undeveloped spur just as the logging road turns uphill to the left. Parking turnoffs before the road ends abruptly at the river.

Trail starts out along the river and then turns inland down an overgrown and often washed out old logging road before wandering to the park boundary in 2 miles.

At the boundary, walk another mile, at least, to the fantastic, beautiful spruce forests around Mosquito Creek. Leave the trail on these flats and just wander amazed at the grandeur here.

Again, some loggers boast that these trees are their long-term logging "reserves." Are they? Should they be? Make your views known.

Bogachiel Rain Forest

Hoh Rain Forest

19   HOH RIVER

A rewarding drive — as pleasant in a drenching winter rain as a summer sun — leads into the rich Olympic rain forest. With the added attraction, in winter, of elk.

Turn east off Highway 101 about 14 miles south of Forks. Drive 19 miles on paved road.

HALL OF MOSSES NATURE TRAIL

A beautiful .75-mile loop through prime examples of moss-draped trees and the lush undergrowth of the climax rain forest.

The trail starts in front of the Hoh Rain Forest Visitor's Center, circling through a grove of towering Sitka spruce into the cathedral-like Hall of Mosses. Plants and trees are marked along the way.

Trail returns to the Visitor's Center.

SPRUCE NATURE TRAIL

No vistas here. Only the quiet splendor of an ancient forest evolving constantly anew out of the past's decay.

A 1.5-mile loop leads away from the crowds through stands of tall spruce and moss-draped groves of vine maples, eventually dropping down to a flat near the Hoh River. Watch for elk in winter.

Trail starts at Visitor's Center. Take fork right at junction with Hall of Mosses trail. Trail returns through another series of groves.

BIG SPRUCE

One of the largest Sitka spruce in Olympic National Park, just off the road.

Watch for signs on the far side of a parking area to the south of the road about 2 miles west of the Hoh Campground. Fourth turnoff from the campground.

The tree, 11-feet 8-inches in diameter and 230 feet tall, is about 500 years old.

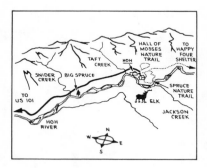

Nature walk, Hoh Rain Forest

Fishing floats and spindrift at Kalaloch

E   THE OLYMPICS, SOUTHWEST

CAMPGROUNDS

Kalaloch — 180 sites. Some overlooking the ocean. Others on forest loops. A crowded campground in summer. Heavily used on weekends even in winter. Clamming, forest walks, beachcombing. Restrooms. Piped water. Summer campground programs. Fee.

Queets River — 26 sites in rain-forest setting along Queets River 14 miles by dirt road from Highway 101. A pleasant but more primitive area than most in the park. Pit toilets. Piped water.

July Creek — 31 sites on the north side of Quinault Lake. Walk-in sites above the lake. No trailers. Although the campground is on the lake there is no recreation use of the lake from the camp. 3.9 miles from Highway 101. Piped water. Restrooms.

Willaby — 19 sites on Quinault Lake. Some sites on lake, others in timber. Restrooms. Piped water. Fee.

Falls Creek — 26 sites on Quinault Lake. Most sites on timber loops. Restrooms. Piped water. Fee.

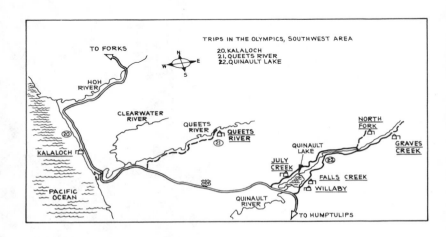

Ruby Beach

North Fork — 8 sites in open wooded area near North Fork of Quinault River. A relatively primitive area. Piped water. Pit toilets. A good place to get away from people. No trailers.
Graves Creek — 45 sites on a single loop in quiet forest. A pleasant, generally uncrowded camp. 20 miles from Highway 101. No trailers.

20 KALALOCH

Glass fishing floats, driftwood, clams, tide pools, eagles, sandpipers, and whales from the longest and most accessible public park beach in the state. As popular in January as it is in July — albeit less crowded.
Drive 35 miles south of Forks on Highway 101.

SEVEN BEACH TRAILS
Walk down any of the seven short — less than .1 mile — trails off Highway 101. Or better yet, take longer hikes on outgoing tides between any of the trails along the 12-mile strip of beach between the Hoh and Quinault Indian Reservations. (Signs on trails may vary from year to year. However, paths follow creeks to the beach in sequence.)
Beach Trails No. 1 and No. 2, south of Kalaloch Campground, lead to long stretches of sand and gravel beach.
Beach Trail No. 4 drops to a heavily used black-sand beach with tide-pool rocks to the north. Surf-fishing and smelting.
Ruby Beach Trail ends at the outlet of Cedar Creek and the sea stacks around Abbey Island. Caves in the rock bluffs to the south. Ford the creek at low tide to hike north.
Beach Trails No. 3, No. 6 and No. 7, all north of Kalaloch Campground, drop to sand and gravel beaches with driftwood havens from the wind. Destruction Island offshore. 🏃

KALALOCH CREEK TRAIL
An easy, pleasant and instructive 2-mile loop up Kalaloch Creek east of Highway 101. Add a rain forest walk to your ocean beach experience.
Trail starts just north of the bridge over Kalaloch Creek which flows between the campground and the Kalaloch Resort. Take care in crossing the highway.
Path skirts the creek for about a half-mile before forking into a loop. Take the trail fork to the left, finding the loop back, to the right, when the path reaches the river near the pumping station. Trail doesn't cross the stream. 🏃

BIG CEDAR
One of the largest Western red cedars in the world — 21 feet in diameter and 130 feet high.
Drive about .6 mile south of the marker to Beach Trail No. 6, watching for a narrow gravel road on the east side of Highway 101. Less than 6 miles north of the Kalaloch Campground. Tree, which actually looks like many trees growing together, is .3 mile from the highway. 🚗

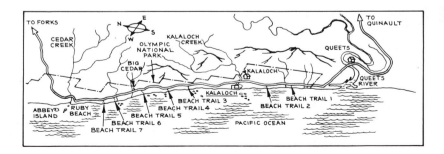

Digging razor clams at Kalaloch

Chanterelle mushroom

Fungus

21   QUEETS RIVER

Upriver views of Olympus, groves of Sitka spruce, and magnificent examples of rain forest in an area generally not overrun with people.

Turn east off Highway 101 about 7 miles south of Queets, driving 14 miles to the end of the road. First view of Olympus in 2 miles. A picturesque grove of Sitka spruce beyond King's Bottom (watch for sign in about 6 miles). ➡

QUEETS RIVER CAMPGROUND LOOP

A single 3-mile loop or two shorter walks on a rain forest trail along streams and across open grass meadows of old abandoned homesteads.

Find the first section of the trail along Sams River at the end of the road on the right about 25 yards back from the ford sign. Trail follows the river and then cuts inland through a series of open meadows. Follow 'T' markers and plastic strips. Walk quietly in winter and watch for elk. Trail returns to the road about 20 yards west of the guard station. About 1.75 miles.

The Queets River section starts east in front of the guard station. Open meadows, groves of spruce, and jungles of moss-laden maple. Trail returns to the road about 30 yards west of the campground entrance. Small signs, about knee high, mark exits. 🧍

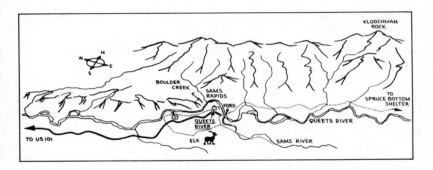

22   QUINAULT LAKE

Rain forest trails, and fern-draped gorges in a rich recreation area off the beaten path.
Forest Service facilities on the South Shore road. National Park facilities on the North Shore road. Both roads join inside the park.

BIG TREE GROVE NATURE TRAIL

A series of loops through rain forest from Willaby Campground with spur trails to Falls Creek Campground, all within Olympic National Forest.

Find trail across the road from parking area just west of Willaby Creek Campground or else out of the west end of the campground. Campground trail crosses Willaby Creek in 500 feet and then turns south beneath the highway.

The joined trails continue south along Willaby Creek past a fern-filled rock gorge to a loop that leads through a "Big Acre" of trees from 150 to 375 years old and then past a "Diorama" area where pictures were prepared for a display in the Museum of Natural History in New York City.

Spur trails to Falls Creek Campground, 2 miles. Watch for signs. 🚶

ENCHANTED VALLEY TRAIL

Almost 11 miles to Enchanted Valley but a half-mile hike down the trail leads to a fern-draped gorge that's enchanting too.

Drive 2.8 miles beyond the Graves Creek Campground to the road end. Trail drops sharply to a bridge across the gorge on the Quinault River.

For best views back up at the fern-covered sides of the 300-foot gorge, find a slippery trail about 30 feet beyond the bridge to a sand bar (at low water) lunch spot. 🚶

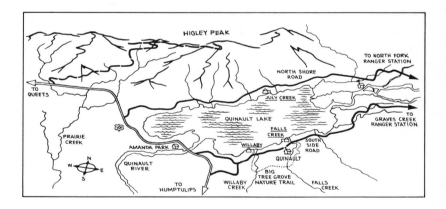

Quinault River and the Enchanted Valley Trail

Mt. Rainier from Klapatche Point

F MT. RAINIER LOOP

The Indians called this mountain God and who's to say they were wrong. Nature here spreads out wonders that never seem to end: Forests, glaciers, flower meadows, canyons, waterfalls, star-burst skies — all fixed by the single spell of the massive peak.

There are no best ways to explore this area. What we list here is only a sample of an inexhaustible supply of things to do, or to simply sit and look at. Every valley, every ridge — every trail sign — offers a new recipe for adventure.

Nor are the mountain's pleasures confined entirely to the National Park. They are most certainly richest there. But the valleys and ridges in National Forest surrounding the park afford — as we list here — equal opportunities to enjoy the mountain.

We urge you to explore everywhere. But wisely. If you are new to mountains, stay on roads and trails. Distances, pitches, and slopes can deceive the eye of the novice. Venture off trails only if you are experienced. And climb ONLY with parties that are trained.

To reach the White River, Sunrise, Tipsoo Lake, Stevens Canyon, and Ohanapecosh side of the mountain drive south from Enumclaw on Highway 410.

To visit the Mowich Lake, Ipsut Creek, Summit Lake area drive to Buckley on Highway 410 west of Enumclaw, continuing south to Wilkeson and Carbonado on Highway 165.

To reach Paradise, the West Side road, the Nisqually Entrance drive from Puyallup south through Eatonville on Highway 161 to the junction of Highway

7 from Tacoma, following park signs from Elbe.

All back country camping in the park is by permit only.

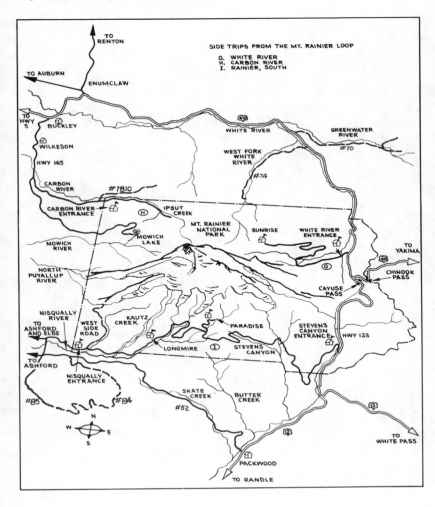

Flower fields near Sunrise Lodge

G WHITE RIVER

High, colorful meadows, brilliant vistas, and deep forest trails in an area often passed over by visitors drawn by the lure of Mt. Rainier National Park.

From Enumclaw, south of Seattle, drive about 25 miles toward Mt. Rainier National Park on Highway 410. All areas listed here lie beyond Federation Forest State Park.

CAMPGROUNDS

The Dalles — 47 units on timbered loops near the White River. Most riverside sites, on a bench above the river, are set aside for trailer campers. Pit toilets. 25 miles from Enumclaw.

Silver Springs — 52 units in open timbered area. Springs bubble from the ground near the road in the center of the loop. Piped water. Pit toilets. 31 miles from Enumclaw.

Corral Pass — 15 units in light subalpine timber. An old CCC development at 5700 feet. Pit toilets. 6 miles from Highway 410 up Corral Pass road No. 7174. Too steep for trailers.

Twin Camps — Primitive camp in subalpine setting at 3700 feet. Piped water. Pit toilets. About 11 miles from Highway 510 via roads No. 70, 7140, and 7030.

White River — 125 sites on wooded loops, a few with views up the White River toward Mt. Rainier. 5 miles from White River Entrance in Mt.

Rainier National Park. Watch for turn-off left beyond White River bridge. Piped water. Restrooms.

Sunrise — 10 units in a walk-in camp about 1.2 miles from the Sunrise parking area, near Shadow Lake. One of the few campgrounds in the state above timberline. Usually closed by snow until mid-July. Always chilly at night. Piped water. Restrooms. Park in the Sunrise parking area about 14.5 miles from the White River Entrance in Mt. Rainier National Park. Park admission.

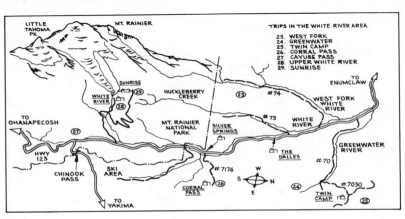

G   WHITE RIVER

23   WEST FORK

Drive to one lookout, hike to another, and tour a loop road that seems to head straight for Mt. Rainier's precipitous Willis Wall.

Drive south from Enumclaw on Highway 410 about 25 miles to The Dalles Campground. Find roads west to Sun Top Lookout off Highway 410 about a mile **north** of the campground and to West Fork road about 4 miles **north** of the campground.

SUN TOP LOOKOUT

Look out at Mt. Rainier from 5270 feet at the end of a road penciled — but wider than it looks — on the side of Sun Top Mountain.

From The Dalles Campground (see above) drive a mile back toward Enumclaw on Highway 410, turning left onto Huckleberry Creek road No. 73, turning left again in about a mile onto lookout road No. 7315. Watch for signs. Lookout 7 miles from the highway.

This lookout is the main attraction on forest tours conducted by the Forest Service in the White River area. Busses even make it to the top.

In addition to arm-length views of Rainier, add Baker, the central Cascades, and on a clear day, the Olympics. Picnic tables and pit toilets at the top. 🚌

LOOP DRIVE

Drive south along the top of Huckleberry Ridge with views straight toward Mt. Rainier, returning down the West Fork road in the valley. A 15-mile loop from Highway 410.

From The Dalles Campground (see above) drive 4 miles back toward Enumclaw on Highway 410, turning left onto road No. 74. In less than 1 mile turn left again onto road No. 75.

The road climbs through a series of heavily-logged areas to Haller Pass at 4650 feet. The road continues along the side of the ridge, gradually dropping down to the valley. Take all turns right until the road reaches No. 74 again. Turn right on No. 74 to return to the highway. 🚗

CLEAR WEST VISTA

An unusual and spectacular view of Mt. Rainier from 5643 feet and almost due north of the mountain. Hike a mile.

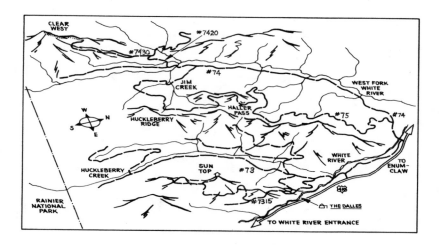

Willis Wall on Mt. Rainier from Clear West Peak

From Highway 410 drive southerly along West Fork road No. 74 (see above) following the road beyond the Jim Creek connection with the Huckleberry Ridge road. (If you drive south on the Huckleberry Ridge road No. 75, turn left on No. 74.)

From road No. 74 turn left onto road No. 7430 in about 1 mile. End of the road about 14 miles away from Highway 410.

At the end of the road, find the unmarked trail uphill and to the left along the edge of the clearcut. Enter forest in about .25 mile. Magnificent vistas of Rainier from the top. To the north, glimpses of Mt. Baker and other Cascade peaks over miles and miles of clearcuts.

Nearest camping

The Dalles, Silver Springs

G WHITE RIVER

24 GREENWATER

Campground tree groves, river-valley hikes, and a steep cliff that challenged pioneers.

Drive south from Enumclaw on Highway 410, turning left in 20 miles (at the log-trestle overpass) onto the Greenwater road No. 70 or continue on Highway 410 to The Dalles Campground. On the right. Watch for signs.

NACHES TRAIL

Visit the "cliff" on the old Naches Trail where pioneers were forced to slaughter mules to get hides for leather ropes in order to lower their wagons down the steep slope.

From Highway 410, drive 8 miles on the Greenwater road No. 70 (see above). Watch for a logging spur to the right just across the Greenwater bridge. (Second concrete bridge.)

Hike a short distance on the best-used spur uphill on the crest of a hogback. (Logging in this private section may disrupt signing.) The old trail is now used heavily by four-wheeled vehicles.

The "cliff" looks deceptively "unsteep" from the bottom. But walk it and find that it's much steeper than it looks. Four-wheeled vehicles can't even climb it without a winch.

GREENWATER LAKES

Hike 2 miles through river-bottom timber along the Greenwater River to the two Greenwater (Meeker) Lakes.

From Highway 410 drive 8 miles easterly on the Greenwater road No. 70 (see above). Watch for trail signs to the right after the road crosses the second concrete bridge over the Greenwater. Logging in this private section may make trail difficult if not impossible to find.

Trails follow the river to two lakes at 2780 and 2846 feet. Timbered lakes. No views.

JOHN MUIR GROVE

A half-mile nature trail winds through a grove of old-growth Douglas fir dedicated to the memory of the famous naturalist by Seattle school children.

Drive south from Enumclaw 25 miles to The Dalles Campground. Find loop trail at the south (upriver) end of the campground out of picnic area. Plants are signed.

In the north end of the campground look for a marked Douglas fir estimated to be more than 700 years old. The tree is 9.5 feet in diameter. 🚶 🚗

Nearest camping
The Dalles, Twin Camp, Silver Springs

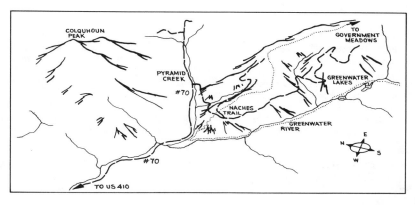

G WHITE RIVER

25 TWIN CAMP

Great country this — mountain-top and meadow vistas highlighted by brilliant color in the fall.

Steep logging roads (no trailers here) lead to a network of high roads that spread to lookout trails, meadows and high drives.

Turn left (east) off Highway 410 onto Greenwater road No. 70 about 4 miles south of Federation State Park (20 miles south of Enumclaw) at a log-trestle overpass. In about 7 miles, turn north onto the Whistler Creek road No. 7140 following it uphill to the old twisty Twin Camp road No. 7030. Twin Camp in about 3 miles.

At Twin Camp turn right onto road No. 7038 for Pyramid Peak and Colquhoun Peak trails. Turn left to Kelly Butte Lookout.

KELLY BUTTE LOOKOUT

Climb a 1.25-mile trail to a lookout atop a bald mountain with expansive views out over the Green River valley toward all major peaks.

At Twin Camp junction (see above) turn left on road No. 7032, driving 4 miles on the narrow spur to its end on the steep, open, south slope of the butte.

A trail, steep the first .25 mile, climbs through open meadows and rock outcrops to a manned lookout on the north edge of the butte. Brilliant flowers in July. Views of Baker, Rainier, Stuart, and other peaks of the Cascade Crest.

COLQUHOUN PEAK TRAIL

Rainier, Baker, Glacier, Stuart, and the tip of Adams from a former lookout site at 5173 feet. A half-mile hike.

At the Twin Camp junction (see above) turn right on road No. 7038, driving about .25 mile before turning right again, uphill, onto signed spur. Road ends at a small parking area in about a half-mile.

The narrow, mossy, and sometimes brushy trail — not often used but easy to follow — leads uphill off the end of the parking area. Best views from the old lookout site atop the mountain. The building has been burned. For other views hike out finger ridges to the south.

PYRAMID PEAK

From Mt. Baker to Mt. Adams with Stuart, Rainier, and other Cascade Crest peaks in between.

From Twin Camp junction (see above) turn right on road No. 7038 and drive 4 miles to Windy Gap on the Pacific Crest Trail. Watch for trail sign on the right. Former lookout site in a half-mile.

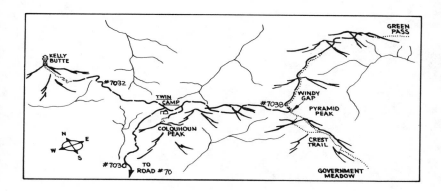

Canadian dogwood

Trail climbs steeply through timber with views reserved for those who complete the trip. The trail-end at 5715 feet affords a prime view of the Cascades to the east. 🚐

GOVERNMENT MEADOW
An easy walk south along the Pacific Crest Trail to a series of open meadows atop the crest. No views. 🚐

At Windy Gap (see Pyramid Lookout above) take Pacific Crest Trail south. Watch for signs.

An easy walk of about 2 miles leads to meadows crossed by the old Naches Trail. Four-wheeled vehicles are barred from meadow areas on Crest Trail although they are allowed on the Naches Trail. Report any transgressions.

CREST DRIVE
From Windy Gap continue another 4 miles easterly by road toward Green Pass. The Crest Trail lies just below the road.

Road wends through timber with only occasional views. Pacific Crest Trail continues toward Green Pass at the end of the road. The pass in about 1.5 more miles by trail. 🚐

Nearest camping
Twin Camp, The Dalles

26   CORRAL PASS

High slopes that glisten with color in the fall. An area used by the army as a winter maneuver area.

From Enumclaw drive southerly about 31 miles to the Silver Springs Campground area, turning left (east) onto the Corral Pass road No. 7174 across from the campground. Watch for sign. Corral Pass in 6 miles. A steep road. No trailers.

RAINIER VIEW (CASTLE MT.) TRAIL

Hike about 1.25 miles to startling views of Mt. Rainier over gnarled and bleached snags atop a ridge at 6050 feet.

At the pass (see above) turn right toward the campground. Find trail (signed) on the right across from a picnic-camp site just before the road drops down to the formal campground in a draw. ⇌

Trail — except for two short, steep pitches, it's a gentle climb — skirts the east side of Castle Mountain (6325) to a saddle where Rainier suddenly fills the sky to the southwest. Trail continues south along the top of the ridge but gets increasingly difficult to follow.

A great place to spend the night. But bring water. Prowl meadows in all directions and climb the ridge toward the top of Castle Mountain for continually better views and glimpses down on meadows below Corral Pass. Tip of Mt. Adams to the southeast. Magnificent on a clear autumn day. Watch for mountain goats too.

FALL COLOR

A spectacle of reds and yellow each fall — before the hunting season begins.

Drive from Highway 410 on Corral Pass road No. 7174 (see above), parking anywhere the color intrigues you or a meadow calls out to be explored. (Don't block the road, however.)

Open slopes below the pass look mostly northwesterly. ⇌

For more high views, hike out a spur roadtrail to the left at the pass toward Noble Knob, an abandoned lookout site in 4 miles. Don't drive the lookout road in a passenger car — for four-wheeled drive vehicles only. Walk the road or prowl open ridges as far as you like for more meadows, more views, and still more color.

Nearest camping

Corral Pass, Silver Springs

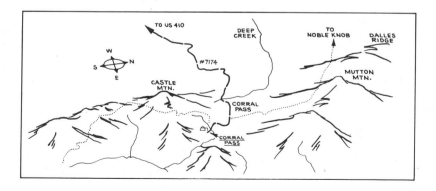

Mt. Rainier from Corral Pass

Upper Tipsoo Lake

27   CAYUSE PASS

Escape down wooded trails along sparkling creeks and noisy rivers for private walks away from the grind and fumes of civilization.

From Enumclaw drive south on Highway 410 to Cayuse Pass in 40 miles. Turn left at the pass for Tipsoo Lakes area. Continue down the highway for Ohanapecosh, Packwood, Randle.

DEER CREEK TRAIL

Hike less than a half-mile past a pretty rockchute waterfall to a timbered valley on Chinook Creek.

From Cayuse Pass (see above) drive south toward Ohanapecosh, watching for a trail sign on the right (extremely difficult to see) between mile posts 12 and 11. Best to drive north from the Stevens Canyon Entrance watching for the sign on the left between mile posts 11 and 12. Park on the east side of the road below the trail.

Trail drops sharply down Deer Creek past a pretty waterfall, branching left at the bottom to Stevens Canyon Entrance (7 miles) or continuing across Chinook Creek to a fork right (uphill to Cayuse Pass) or straight ahead to Owyhigh Lakes in 5 miles. 🚶

EAST SIDE TRAIL

Walk 4.5 miles downhill from Cayuse Pass, returning to the highway up the Deer Creek Trail (above).

From Cayuse Pass drive south to the large parking area on the right, just below the junction. Find the trail off the highway to the right about 15 yards beyond the parking area.

The trail, a continuation of the trail from Tipsoo Lakes (see below), drops down the upper reaches of Chinook Creek to a junction with the Deer Creek-Owyhigh Lakes Trail. Turn left, crossing the creek, to climb back to the highway or continue down river to Stevens Canyon Entrance in 10.7 more miles. 🚶

TIPSOO LAKE TRAIL

A pleasant 1.5-mile hike from Tipsoo Lakes down to Highway 123 below Cayuse Pass on a trail little used by the general public.

Find the trail off the Pacific Crest Trail across the highway from Tipsoo Lake.

The trail slopes steeply downhill (best to hike it in that direction), pretty much following a stream bed to Highway 123 about .4 mile below Cayuse. Path passes through hemlock, subalpine fir, and floral displays (at their best in August). 🚶

Nearest camping
White River, Ohanapecosh

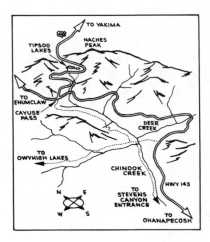

G WHITE RIVER

28 UPPER WHITE RIVER

Hike out a pretty mountain ridge, down to two secluded lakes, or to a glacier strewn with avalanche debris.

From Enumclaw drive south on Highway 410 about 38 miles, turning right at signs indicating the White River Entrance to Mt. Rainier National Park. White River Campground 7 miles from the entrance station at the end of a spur road up the White River. Watch for sign. Sunrise Point Viewpoint 13 miles beyond the entrance station. ⬛

SUNRISE RIDGE

Hike out a little-used trail atop the ridge northeast of the Sunrise Point parking area to views back at Rainier, signs of elk, and — if you're lucky — a golden eagle or two.

From the Sunrise Point parking area (see above) find trail to Sunrise and Clover Lakes (see below), continuing along the top of the ridge after the main trail turns left downhill.

Trail wends through subalpine timber, breaking out into high, open meadows in about 1 mile. Views also of the Goat Rocks, the Cascades, and down to the White River. Stay on the trail, preserving the meadows for others. ⭫

SUNRISE AND CLOVER LAKES

Drop sharply downhill, remembering you must climb up again, to pretty lakes out of sight of the mountain. About 1.1 mile.

From the Sunrise Point parking area take the well-marked trail out the ridge, turning downhill in about .25 mile. Trail drops from about 6000 to 5700 feet.

Instant seclusion once you leave the parking area. The trail passes Sunrise Lake first, then crosses patches of meadow to Clover Lake. Hike on to the Palisades Lakes, 3.7 miles from the parking area. ⭫

EMMONS GLACIER

Look down on the dirty snout of Emmons Glacier and note the huge boulders that were "sailed" down the glacier from Little Tahoma (the nubbin' peak to Rainier's left) on an avalanche cushion of air.

Find Glacier Basin trail at the upper end of the White River Campground (see above). Hike about 1 mile before turning left on a glacier moraine spur. Hike along top of moraine as far as you wish.

Boulders on the ice and dust-debris atop some rocks along the moraine were

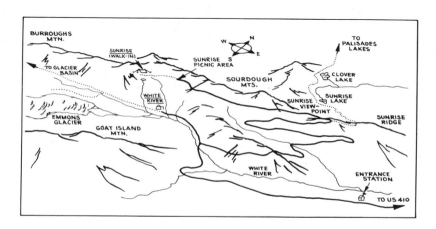

Snout of the Emmons Glacier

deposited when a huge slab toppled off Little Tahoma in December, 1963, and plummeted down onto Emmons Glacier at speeds estimated by some up to 300 miles an hour. Air trapped beneath the plunging debris buoyed it up, carrying rocks 4 miles down the ice and to within 2000 feet of the White River Campground. ⚐

Nearest camping
   White River, Sunrise Walk-in Camp

Mt. Rainier from Dege Peak

29 SUNRISE

Hike across flower meadows spread beneath Mt. Rainier like a brilliantly-woven carpet with views...on views...on views.

From Enumclaw drive south on Highway 410 about 38 miles, turning right to the White River Entrance of Mt. Rainier National Park. Continue past the entrance station to the end of the paved road in 15 miles at 6500 feet.

Only the highlight-hikes to be taken in the immediate area are listed here. For more details and more trips obtain a trail map of the area at the Sunrise Visitor Center.

DEGE PEAK

Take the heavily-used trail uphill out of the upper picnic area, turning right near the top of Sourdough Mountain ridge and following the trail through seemingly endless flower meadows to the 7006-foot peak in 1.4 mile. Either return the way you came or take trail down to the highway, another .7 mile, to be met by car.

FREMONT LOOKOUT

Turn left at the top of the uphill trail (see Dege Peak above) and hike west along the ridge to Frozen Lake. Turn right at fork just beyond the lake. Manned lookout in 2.8 miles from the campground. Note small bits of pumice thrown out by an eruption of the mountain. Views of Rainier, Grand Park, and down Lodi Creek.

FOREST LAKE

Turn left at the top of the uphill trail and hike only a few hundred yards to a spur right that leads over Sourdough Mountain ridge. Trail drops sharply through a series of meadows to the timbered lake at 5669 feet. No views of the mountain. Not many take this trail. So find privacy — even on a busy weekend — in these out-of-the-way meadows.

EMMONS VISTA NATURE TRAIL

Look down on the Emmons Glacier and out at Rainier and Little Tahoma (the small peak just to Rainier's left) from a trail describing plants and mountain features.

Find trailhead across the road from Sunrise Lodge, next to the graveled road. Follow numbered stakes to Emmons Vista overlook with view of the largest glacier on Mt. Rainier. See also the destruction wrought by the rockfall from Little Tahoma. Round trip 1.8 mile.

To hike 2.6 miles downhill to White River Campground take the first fork to the right on the nature trail (above), keeping left at the next trail junction. Spur also leads to Shadow Lake and lower campground in about 1 mile.

BURROUGHS MOUNTAIN

No doubt that you are in alpine country here. Views in every direction, certainly. But it's the ground-hugging, delicate plants that tell the main story.

Take the uphill trail (see Dege Peak above), turn left, continue past the Fremont Lookout turnoff, and then climb uphill to the left. Memorial marker to Edmond S. Meany, long-time president of The Mountaineers.

After soaking up the 360-degree panorama (it will take awhile), either return the way you came, drop down to Glacier Basin (the most ambitious route) to White River Campground, or continue on around First Burroughs Mountain back to Sunrise.

Nearest camping

Sunrise, White River

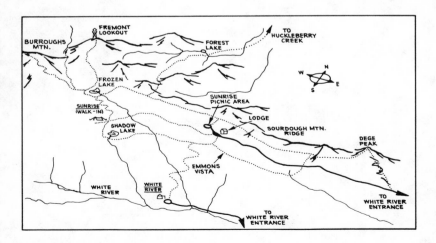

H   CARBON RIVER

Lakes, lookouts, waterfalls, and forest trails — some in Mt. Rainier National Park, others in Snoqualmie National Forest.

From Buckley (on Highway 410 between Sumner and Enumclaw, south of Seattle) drive on Highway 410 to the southwest corner of town, turning left onto Highway No. 162-165 toward Wilkeson, Carbonado, and Orting. Turn left again in 1.5 miles onto Highway 165.

Highway 165 goes through old coal-mining towns of Wilkeson and Carbonado before heading up the Carbon River toward the mountain.

Junction to Mowich Lake and Carbon River Entrance to the park about 5 miles south of Wilkeson. Follow Highway 165 right to Mowich Lake. 12 miles to the lake and 5 miles to the park boundary from the junction.

Continue along the Carbon River to Carbon River Entrance and Snoqualmie Forest roads.

CAMPGROUNDS

Ipsut Creek — 32 sites on loop in pleasant timber area. Open May to October. Busy on weekends. Evening programs on weekends. Pit toilets. Piped water. 18 miles from Wilkeson.

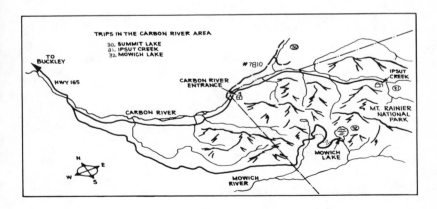

H   CARBON RIVER

30   SUMMIT LAKE

Hike to a meadow-circled lake with views of Mt. Rainier, climb to a lookout site, or drive to lakes and viewpoints just outside the National Park boundary.

From Buckley (on Highway 410 between Sumner and Enumclaw) drive on Highway 410 to the southwest corner of town, turning left on Highway No. 162-165 to Wilkeson, Carbonado, and Orting, turning left again in 1.5 miles on Highway 165 to Wilkeson and Carbonado.

Continue 18 miles on Carbon River road, following signs to Ipsut Creek and Fairfax. Turn left onto road No. 7810 just before the Carbon River road reaches the entrance to Mt. Rainier National Park.

Logging has been extremely heavy in this part of Snoqualmie National Forest. Vistas yield to new clearcuts almost every year. Some contend the logging was purposely conducted here just to box in Mt. Rainier National Park. Look at it yourself and judge.

SUMMIT LAKE TRAIL
Hile 2.5 miles to Summit Lake, tucked into a crater-like pocket atop a mountain at 5440 feet and surrounded by colorful flower meadows.

From the Carbon River road (see above) follow road No. 7810 to a T junction in about 6 miles, turning left. Find trail to Summit Lake, Twin Lake, and Bearhead Mountain at the end of the spur.

Trail starts to the left, uphill, through a clearcut before ducking into timber. At Twin Lake (4880) take trail fork to the left (trail to right leads to Bearhead Mountain). Trail starts steeply from Twin Lake, then levels into a long traverse to Summit Lake.

At Summit Lake, hike to the right for a series of camp spots in small meadows, glimpses from the edge of the crater ridge down on Lily and Coundly Lakes (no trails), and views over Summit Lake at Mt. Rainier.

Hike to the left for views over the edge toward Rainier. Primitive camp spots everywhere. Bear grass mixed with glacier lilies and snow in late July.

BEARHEAD MOUNTAIN
From 6089 feet look down on everything except, of course, Mt. Rainier.

Take trail to Summit Lake (see above), turning right at junction at the first small (Twin) lake. Plan to rest awhile at the meadow-rimmed pond, not that you'll be tired, but simply because it's a quiet, pleasant place to be.

After traversing through forest on the side of the mountain, the trail switchbacks to a saddle and an unmarked trail junction.

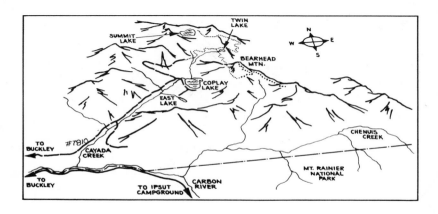

Carbon River valley and Mt. Rainier from Cayada Creek road

Take the uphill path to the left which climbs through a whole series of gaudy flower meadows to the site of the former lookout tower. Spectacular views down on Summit Lake and out on a sky filled with Rainier. Places to camp. No water, just vistas.

COPLAY/EAST LAKES
Two small mountain lakes at about 4000 feet that were once tucked into deep forest.

From the Carbon River road drive about 6 miles on road No. 7810 to a T intersection, turning right to Coplay Lake and then on, turning right again, to East Lake.

When this guide was first written, both lakes were surrounded by rich forest. Take a look now. Despite promises by the Forest Service to protect lakes, these two have been logged to the shoreline.

The logging on the shore of Coplay was designated as a "partial cut," but the destruction, you'll find, has been total.

In its environmental assessment, the agency said the logging would "enhance the outdoor activities of lake users." Make your own judgment.

Nearest camping
Ipsut Creek

H CARBON RIVER

31 IPSUT CREEK

Waterfalls, rain forest-like trails, and a lake.

From Buckley (on Highway 410 between Enumclaw and Sumner) drive on Highway 410 to the southwest corner of town, turning sharply left onto Highway 162-165 to Wilkeson, Carbonado, and Orting, turning left again in 1.5 miles to Highway 162 through Wilkeson and Carbonado.

Entrance to Mt. Rainier National Park on the Carbon River road in 19 miles.

RAIN FOREST LOOP

Technically not a rain forest. Olympic National Park reserves the rain forest name for its dank sections on the west side of the peninsula. But the Mt. Rainier version is so close only an expert can tell the difference.

Find trail to the right in front of the park's Carbon River Entrance Station (see above). Trail loops a half-mile around June Creek. The main trail — the loop branches left in .2 mile — continues along the western border of the park. Fat skunk cabbage, mosses, and lots of sprawling devils club.

CHENUIS FALLS

Chenuis Creek foams over moss-bordered craggy rock-slab slides. A .2-mile walk.

Watch for trail sign on the left (river side) of the road about 3.5 miles beyond the park entrance station (see above).

Course of the path varies from year to year as spring floods wipe out old paths and the river finds constantly new courses. A temporary bridge crosses the river to the established trail. Trail continues past the falls another 3 miles, but goes nowhere in particular. A pleasant walk, however.

GREEN LAKE TRAIL

A steep 2 miles to a wooded mountain lake. But a 1-mile hike leads to pretty Ranger Falls on Ranger Creek.

From the park entrance station drive about 2 miles up the Carbon River, watching for Green Lake trail sign on the right.

Trail winds up a series of switchbacks through deep forest to the lake in a tight timbered bowl. No views. Watch for a marked spur trail to the left about halfway up for a view of the falls, stringing down moss-green cliffs.

Nearest camping

Ipsut Creek

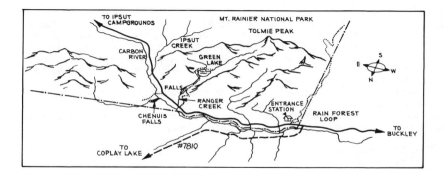

Chenuis Falls

32 MOWICH LAKE

Meadow vistas, waterfalls, and lakes all near 5000 feet.

Drive through Buckley (between Enumclaw and Sumner) on Highway 410 to the southwest corner of town, turning sharply left onto Highway 162-165 to Wilkeson and Orting. Turn left again in 1.5 miles to Highway 162.

To reach Mowich Lake turn off the river road following Highway 162, about 5 miles south of Wilkeson (the first right turn after crossing the high green bridge), driving another 12.5 miles on a scenic but gravel road.

Mowich Lake road

Heavy use creates constant, unsolved problems for this gem of a lake. The Park Service improved the road to make the lake easier to visit and then tried to close it when too many came. The road is open again now. But all of the problems remain.

Camping is confined now to a barren, uninviting parking lot. Vehicle camping barred.

To help ease the pressures here, stay on trails and treat the meadows with extreme care.

EUNICE LAKE

Take your own calendar picture of Mt. Rainier reflected in the chill blue of a mountain lake surrounded by flower meadows. A 2.1-mile walk.

At Mowich Lake (see above) start at sign off road or follow tourist path to the left from the parking area to a trail along the west shore of the lake. Trail climbs slightly and then traverses a ridge to a junction just below Ipsut Pass (5100 feet). Turn left to Eunice Lake. But first walk another 25 yards for views down Ipsut Creek. The trail to the lake drops below a bluff before climbing back to the lake at 5355 feet.

At the lake, pick your own "best view" from thousands. Many follow the trail to the left around the lake to a viewpoint just at the base of the mountain below Tolmie Peak Lookout.

To reach the lookout, hike another mile steeply uphill by trail. ⴕ

SPRAY FALLS

A sparkling veil of water tumbles over one cliff, turns, and floods over another. About 2 miles.

Find trail to the right off the end of the parking area at Mowich Lake (see above).

As the trail starts to switchback steeply upward, watch for a marked spur to the right which leads to the falls in about .3 mile. Spur ends at the falls. Main trail continues another .5 mile to flower meadows at Spray Park. ⴕ

Nearest camping
Ipsut Creek

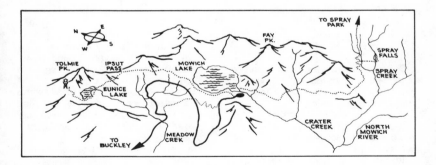

Mt. Rainier and Nisqually Glacier

I RAINIER, SOUTH

Drive across the southern shoulder of Mt. Rainier through low valleys and over high ridges with ever-changing views of the mountain.

But to know the mountain, enjoy the meadows, and appreciate the rich silence of the valleys — park your car, get out, and walk.

To reach the Nisqually Entrance, drive south from Seattle to Puyallup, continuing south on Highway 161 to Eatonville and a junction with Highway 7 from Tacoma. Turn onto Highway 706 at Elbe. Park entrance in 13 miles from Elbe.

CAMPGROUNDS

Sunshine Point — 22 sites on a lightly-timbered river bar about .2 mile from Nisqually Entrance. View of Rainier. Open year around. Piped water in summer. Boil river water in winter. Pit toilets.

Longmire — (open May to mid-June for overflow camping only) 132 sites on timbered loops 6 miles from Nisqually Entrance. Piped water. Restrooms.

Cougar Rock — 200 sites on several wooded loops 8 miles from Nisqually Entrance. Piped water. Restrooms. Evening programs.

Ohanapecosh—See page 143.

Big Creek — 30 tent and trailer sites in the national forest just outside Mt. Rainier National Park. Turn south from Highway 706 onto a forest road about 3 miles west of the park entrance. Turn left beyond the bridge. Campground in a half-mile.

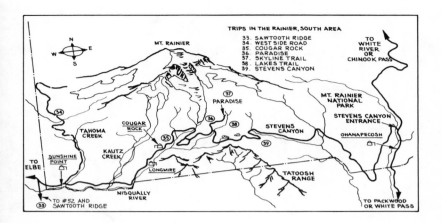

33   SAWTOOTH RIDGE

A handful of pretty mountain lakes guarded by a high-rock lookout with an exploding view of Mt. Rainier. All just outside the national park.

Turn south off Highway 706 onto forest road No. 52 (to Packwood) about 10 miles east of Elbe and 3 miles west of the park entrance.

Cross the Nisqually River and then turn left (east) continuing past the Big Creek Campground on road No. 52 to a junction with road No. 84 in about 3 miles.

BERTHA MAY LAKE

Visit three lakes along one trail. In less than 2 miles.

To find the trail, drive south on road No. 84 at the intersection of road No. 52 with 84 (see above) turning right onto Teeley Creek road No. 8410 in about a mile. Trailhead in 4 more miles.

Path climbs over a slight ridge to Pothole Lake in about a half-mile, up a ridge to Bertha May Lake in .75 mile or less, and over still another ridge to Granite Lake in a half-mile.

Camping spots near all of the lakes. For one with a view of Mt. Rainier, too, hike to the outlet at the east end of Granite Lake. If you tire of looking at the mountain there, turn and watch the birds on the lake.

CORA LAKE

Hike uphill just .75 mile to a pretty lake tucked below High Rock Lookout with glimpses of Mt. Rainier.

Find the trail (signed as Big Creek Trail) about a mile from road No. 84 on spur No. 8420. Turn right on the spur road about 5 miles from the 84/52 junction.

Path starts uphill to the south on an old roadway and then passes a couple of small waterfalls as it switches up to the lake. Formal campsites.

Views of Mt. Rainier through the trees as the trail crests at the lake.

HIGH ROCK LOOKOUT

From an abandoned lookout perched on the prow of a cliff pay homage to Rainier, Adams and what's left of St. Helens.

Drive 10 miles from the 84/52 intersection on road No. 84 to Towhead Gap. Find the trail uphill on the right. Starting in a clearcut, the path follows the ridge steadily upward. (You can see the lookout perched on its rock from the road.) Occasional

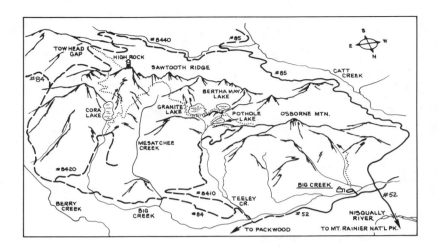

vistas through the trees but the best views are reserved for the top at 5685 feet.

The Forest Service no longer maintains the lookout, but unknown hikers who love the place still do, replacing windows and cleaning the building every year. Join them in trying to keep the place intact.

Give yourself enough time to soak up all the vistas and watch the marmots scurry around ledges on the cliffs.

34   WEST SIDE

Meet the mountain over the top of a lake, from a roadside leading to a waterfall, and above one of its most recent displays of power.

Paved road continues on to Longmire, Paradise, etc.

From the Nisqually Entrance Station drive less than 1 mile to turn left up the West Side Road, open to the end at the North Puyallup River.

Best road view where the road turns east above the river at the foot of Klapatche Ridge.

Gravel all the way. The paved road continues on to Longmire, Paradise, etc.

DENMAN FALLS

Walk less than .25 mile down St. Andrews Creek to a pretty waterfall. But don't miss the fine example of a stonemason's art on the way.

Drive north on the West Side Road (see above) about 11 miles to St. Andrews Creek. Park south of the bridge and find trail to the falls on the left, downstream.

To view the bridge, walk down the stone stairway on the lower side of the structure. The stairway, which drops to the creek's edge, was built just so you could admire the stonemason's effort.

Continue downstream to an overlook point above the falls. But don't bother to go any farther down the trail. Some books list two more falls downstream but the steep trail, ending in a clearcut at the park boundary, doesn't go near either one.

Trail across the bridge and uphill to the right climbs to Klapatche Park.

LAKE GEORGE

An easy trail, less than 1 mile, winds to a secluded lake offering glimpses of Rainier from its west shore.

High Rock Lookout

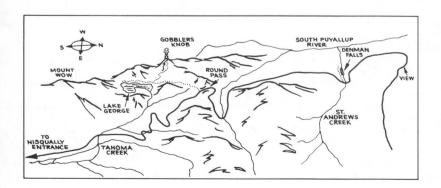

Lake George

Drive up the West Side Road about 7 miles, watching for parking area and signs on the left.

At the lake, find fisherman trails to the right along the far shore for views of the mountain. Continue on the trail another 1.5 miles to lookout on Gobblers Knob. 🚶

(Drive a short distance beyond the trail parking area to a memorial to Marines killed in a 1946 plane crash on the mountain.)

KAUTZ CREEK MUDFLOW

A desolation of dead trees attests to the awesome power of mud — some 50 million cubic yards of it.

From the Nisqually Entrance drive 3.6 miles toward Longmire, watching for a formal display on the right beyond Kautz Creek.

A self-guiding trail, starting at the formal display, identifies highlights of the catastrophe, triggered by heavy rains on new snow, that sent a wall of water, ice, and mud hurtling down the mountain from Kautz Glacier. The old road lies under 50 feet of mud. Dead trees were suffocated and choked by the girdling flow. 🚶 🚗

Nearest camping

Sunshine Point, Cougar Rock

35   COUGAR ROCK

Escape — but not entirely — from the overpowering mountain to more intimate beauties of forest trails, waterfalls, and quiet, springfed meadows.

From the Nisqually Entrance Station drive to Longmire, Cougar Rock Campground, and Narada Falls on road to Paradise. 🛉

TRAIL OF SHADOWS

Hundreds walk these trails past soda springs almost every summer day. But the lushness of the meadows quiets all but the laughter of children.

Find a well-worn nature trail across from the Longmire Inn. It's the only trail likely to be open in May and June while others are still covered by snow. Walk a half-mile past a capped formal soda spring and around a lush marsh fed by 50 uncapped springs, some heated to 85 degrees.

And please! DON'T feed the deer. You act most kindly by ignoring their pleas. Deer summered on crackers, bread crusts, and cigarettes cannot survive a winter. 🛉 ⇥

COUGAR ROCK TO LONGMIRE

Drop below the highway for an easy, peaceful stroll downhill accompanied by the quiet song of the Nisqually River.

From the Cougar Rock Campground find the Wonderland Trail across the road, about 100 yards downhill from the campground entrance.

The 1.7-mile trail ends at the Visitor Center at Longmire.

CARTER FALLS

From one waterfall walk past another down the Paradise River.

From the Nisqually Entrance, drive 14 miles to the parking area near Narada Falls. Follow the trail past Narada Falls, continuing downhill on the Wonderland Trail past Carter Falls to Cougar Rock Campground.

To walk upsteam (Carter Falls in 1 mile) find Wonderland Trail off the end of a spur road just across from the campground entrance. Trail goes past the side of a house at the end of the road.

Note wire-wrapped wooden pipes between Carter Falls and Cougar Rock. They once carried water downstream to a power generator at the house. 🛉

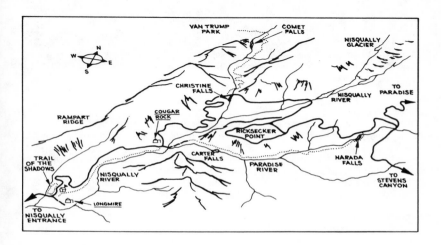

Comet Falls

COMET FALLS

A fork of Van Trump Creek plumes 320 feet over a cliff just off the trail.But don't miss the big bowl etched by the creek in rock just upstream of the trail bridge less than .25 mile from the highway.

From the Nisqually Entrance drive 10.3 miles toward Paradise, finding the trail off a parking area just before the road passes below Christine Falls.

Trail climbs constantly and continually to the falls. Trail ends at Van Trump Park, 2.3 miles from the road. A steady climb all the way. ⫯

Nearest camping

Cougar Rock, Longmire

Paradise Visitor Center and Tatoosh Range

36 PARADISE

No place was ever more truly named. An idyl unequalled anywhere of color, cloud, and snow spread lavishly below a grand Rainier.

From the Nisqually Entrance drive 18 miles to the visitor center-lodge complex. From the Stevens Canyon Entrance drive 24 miles up the Stevens Canyon road.

The summer season is short here, but wildly spectacular. Snow gives way within a day to fields of avalanche and glacier lilies. And other flowers follow in a rolling procession of color that lasts into autumn, when summer colors yield to the reds and yellows of fall.

Blooming follows no fixed yearly schedule. Often the high meadows remain covered with snow until mid-July, with the most brilliant displays of flowers during the first 2 weeks of August. But it varies each year. Avoid the first two Sundays in August. Cars then are often parked back 2 miles. No crowds mid-week, however. ⵌ

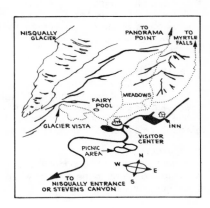

MEADOW TRAILS
Glimpse a corner of paradise from sidewalk trails designed for baby buggies, street shoes, and even high heels.

Paved trails criss-cross all the meadows between the Visitor Center and the Paradise Inn. Pick your own. And one is no better than another. Each has its own special offering of flowers, wildlife, or vista. 🏃 🚐

One plea, though. Stay on the formal paths. If every visitor here decided to romp through the flowers there'd soon be no meadows left.

NISQUALLY GLACIER VISTA
For a special view down on the Nisqually Glacier walk an easy 1-mile round trip through meadows and past a Fairy Pool. 🏃 🚐

Take a heavily-used trail uphill to the left of the Visitor Center. Watch for signs. Turn left in less than 50 yards. Trail loops along the edge of a bluff for views down on the snout of the glacier, and up the 3-mile-long river of ice.

VISITOR CENTER
The unique design remains controversial but few complain of the features inside the Visitor Center.

Find displays on the geology, ecology, and climbing history of the mountain. Ranger-naturalists start nature walks from the center and present programs inside. Walk up the circling ramp to a lounge with broad views of the meadows and peak. Food service, too. 🏃

Nearest camping
Cougar Rock, Ohanapecosh

37 SKYLINE TRAIL

Follow spring up the mountain from Paradise.

From the Paradise Visitor Center hike 5.7 miles round trip, climbing 1500 feet, to Panorama Point and views of Nisqually Glacier, Rainier, and over your shoulder, Adams, Hood, and a little of what's left of St. Helens.

Start either at the Visitor Center or behind the Paradise Ranger Station. Follow signs. Return the same way or continue east on the main trail, returning to the Center via a spur trail (watch for sign) at Golden Gate. 🚐

MORAINE TRAIL
Take a half-mile spur onto the moraine along the edge of Nisqually Glacier and flower fields that bloom late in August.

Turn west off the Skyline Trail about .7 mile from the Visitor Center.

Look down at the glacier but don't venture out on it unless you are properly equipped and trained. The inviting white slope hides a treacherous array of crevasses. 🏃

GLACIER VISTA
On a warm day watch and listen to the moving river of ice.

Hike about a half-mile beyond the Moraine Trail junction (see above) to a rock bluff overlooking the crevasse fields of the Nisqually.

The glacier moves about one foot a day with each inch of progress marked by crashing ice pinnacles and plunging rock. 🏃

PANORAMA POINT
A small meadow at 7000 feet with a big view. Often best between 6 and 8 in the morning and after 5 in the evening when Adams, Hood, and the shell of St. Helens stand out most clearly.

Edith Creek and Tatoosh Range

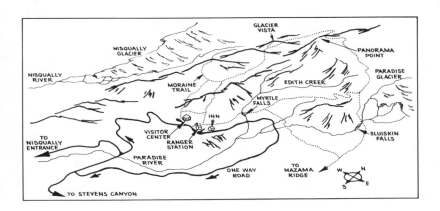

Avalanche lilies

From the Visitor Center, hike 2.5 miles; from the Ranger Station, the same.
The temptation is great here to leave the trails and wander over the rocky talus slopes seeking fresher vistas. But watch the weather. Fog can quickly fill the valley and creep up the slope. If you see fog moving in, return to the trail. 🚶

Nearest camping
Cougar Rock, Ohanapecosh

38 LAKES TRAIL

Two waterfalls, flower meadows one after the other, reflecting pools, and a whole series of small mountain lakes.
From the Paradise Ranger Station take trails pointing to the Ice Caves and Reflection Lakes. Hike to Reflection Lakes on the Stevens Canyon road to be picked up by

car, a 3.1-mile walk. Or else a complete loop to Reflection Lakes and back to Paradise in 5 miles.

MYRTLE FALLS

Walk a half-mile from the Ranger Station across the superb flower fields in Edith Creek Basin to Myrtle Falls.

Just before the bridge crosses above the falls, drop down a dusty trail about 150 feet to a view of the falls with Rainier in the background.

Continue past the falls for still more flower fields and views up at Sluiskin Falls, named after an Indian guide who aided Hazard Stevens and P. B. Van Trump in the first recorded climb of Rainier in 1870. Follow the main trail, left, atop Mazama Ridge for a spur trip to Stevens-Van Trump Monument and Sluiskin Falls. (Trail spur also leads to Paradise Ice Caves.)

MAZAMA RIDGE

Flower fields alternate with small lakes and groves of alpine trees on this downhill spur to Reflection Lakes.

Turn right at the Mazama Ridge junction (see above). Reflection Lakes in 2 miles. Or start from the Stevens Canyon Road finding the trail north of the highway between Reflection and Louise Lakes.

Watch here for colorful displays of bear grass and western anemone. (Bear grass some years, however, makes hardly any showing at all here or elsewhere in the park.)

Pause at Faraway Rock, a bluff overlooking Lake Louise and Reflection Lakes. And watch for the reflection of the mountain in every small pool along the trail.

Nearest camping
Cougar Rock, Ohanapecosh

39 STEVENS CANYON

Walk to the sudden seclusion of two lakes and a waterfall or look down into a deep canyon from rock slabs scoured by glaciers.

From Paradise continue east on the Stevens Canyon road to the Stevens Canyon Entrance and Highway 123 and 410. Or from the Stevens Canyon Entrance drive toward Paradise.

A "must" drive whenever the road is open. Best, perhaps, in autumn when hillsides explode with splashes of red and yellow leaves. Road closed in winter.

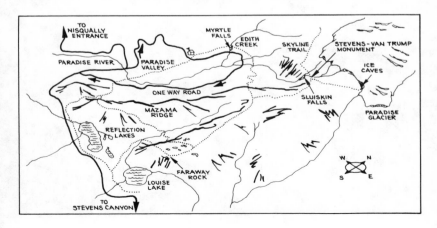

Striations, scratches, made by the glacier passing over rock at Box Canyon

SNOW AND BENCH LAKES

Whistle with marmots across soggy meadows on a trail to two lakes less than 1 mile from the road.

Drive east from Paradise down Stevens Canyon road, watching for trail and small turnout on the right about 1 mile beyond Louise Lake.

Trail climbs sharply through brush to open meadows above Bench Lake, then swings right to a small ridge, still more meadows, and Snow Lake.

Marmots and picas (rock conies) galore. Shooting stars and elephant head flowers in soggy creek beds. Snow at the upper end of Snow Lake until late August most years.

And don't be discouraged if it's raining. The intimate splendors of the meadows make up for loss of Rainier's presence.

BOX CANYON

The time of man amounts to less than an instant here amid the still-unfinished efforts of persistent nature.

From Paradise drive down the Stevens Canyon road about 11 miles to the Muddy Fork of the Cowlitz and a formal nature display on the right. From Stevens Canyon Entrance drive toward Paradise about 12.7 miles, display on the left.

Find trail along the edge of the deep canyon uphill across from the formal display. Trail loops .25 mile across a footbridge, returning to the highway. Rock slabs show grinding footprints of an ancient glacier. The 180-foot canyon demonstrates the power of a stream — and time.

At trail junction uphill turn right and hike about 1 mile on the Wonderland Trail to a shelter on Nickel Creek. Generally occupied.

MARTHA FALLS

Walk less than a mile to enjoy a refreshing respite at the base of a noisy waterfall.

Take the Wonderland Trail off the Stevens Canyon road (downhill to the east) about a mile below the Bench Lake trailhead.

The path drops across the base of the waterfall. Lots of resting and watching rocks nearby.

Nearest camping

Ohanapecosh, Cougar Rock

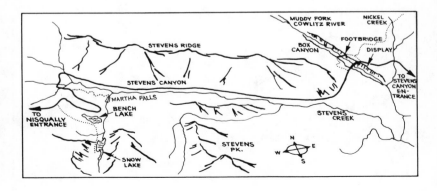

J AMERICAN RIVER

Flower-meadow walks, reflected mountains, roaring waterfalls, and a soda spring along the American and Bumping Rivers.

Drive south from Enumclaw on Highway 410 over Cayuse and Chinook Passes. 20 miles from Chinook Pass to the Bumping River road.

CAMPGROUNDS

Lodgepole — 30 sites in stand of short lodgepole pine. Some sites oriented to the river. Pit toilets. 8.3 miles from Chinook Pass. Well water. Fee.

Pleasant Valley — 18 sites in flat open areas south of the highway. Heavy trailer use. 11.8 miles from Chinook Pass. Pit toilets.

Hells Crossing — 16 sites all well-separated in open timber area on the river. Park on campground road spur and carry gear to table and tent sites. Pit toilets. Well water. 15 miles from Chinook Pass. Fee.

Pine Needle — 6 sites on narrow flat strip along the river. Road follows the top of a ridge before dropping down to the camp. Pit toilet. 20.8 miles from Chinook Pass.

American Fork — 13 sites stretched out along American River. Some near river. Some in timber. Busy camp. Just across the bridge on the Bumping River road. Pit toilets. Federal fee.

Cedar Spring — 18 sites. Usually busy. Almost a part of the American Fork Campground but on the Bumping River. Pit toilets.

Soda Springs — 26 sites in pleasant open timber along the Bumping River. Most sites oriented to the river. 4.8 miles from Highway 410. Pit toilets. Well water. Fee.

Cougar Flats — 9 sites on a secluded loop away from river. Day-use picnic area along the river. 6 miles from Highway 410. Pit toilets. Well water. Fee.

Bumping Crossing — 7 sites just off the road. 9.5 miles from Highway 410. An undefined camp. Pit toilets.

Bumping Dam — 31 units on flat wooded area below Bumping Dam. 11.4 miles from Highway 410. Drive over top of dam to reach campground. Pit toilets. Water.

Bumping Lake — 39 units in new campground off east shore of lake. Continue on road No. 174 about a half-mile beyond dam. Pit toilets. Well water. Fee.

Deep Creek — 6 sites in a deep forest loop at the end of road No. 162. Primarily a horse camp. 20.3 miles from Highway 410. Pit toilets.

Granite Lake — 8 sites on a pretty alpine lake. Some in the open. Others in shade. Pit toilets. 17.5 miles from Highway 410.

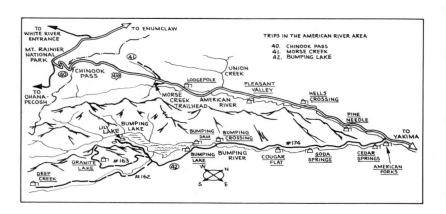

Union Falls

Chinook Pass and Naches Peak

40 CHINOOK PASS

One of the few unspoiled passes in the state — no ski slopes, no hamburger stands, no helicopter rides, not even a service station. Nothing, in fact, but beauty, beauty, and still more beauty.

Turn east on Highway 410 at Cayuse Pass and drive to Chinook Pass on the crest of the Cascades and at the boundary between Mt. Rainier National Park and Wenatchee National Forest. 🚗

CREST LOOP TRAIL

Hike 3 miles across high meadows with views first to the east and then to the west and Mt. Rainier. An easy refreshing trip.

Start at the wooden trail bridge over the highway north of Tipsoo Lake area, hike south around Naches Peak, and return to Tipsoo on the Pacific Crest Trail (Alternate).

Views going south of the American River valley over occasional small ponds. Trail joins the Crest Trail west of the ridge. More open flower meadows on return trail going north with views of Rainier reflected in more small ponds. Particularly colorful in the fall. 🚶

TIPSOO LAKE WALKS

Join thousands by taking pictures of Rainier reflected in Tipsoo Lake. Walk trails on the east side of the lake. For more unusual views, go south of the road to less-pictured lakes, just as pretty.

Smaller lakes lie just east of the Pacific Crest Trail on a bench above the highway. Hike anywhere across open meadows for your own "best" picture. 🚶

SHEEP LAKE

A 2-mile hike leads to a pretty open meadow lake at 5700 feet.

Follow the Pacific Crest Trail north from the overhead trail bridge at Chinook Pass.

Trail traverses Yakima Peak above the highway before climbing gradually to the lake. Views down on the American River valley and out on peaks of Cascade Crest from meadows above the lake. A very popular family hike. Trail continues to Sourdough Gap and Crystal Mountain ski area.

Nearest camping

Lodgepole, Ohanapecosh

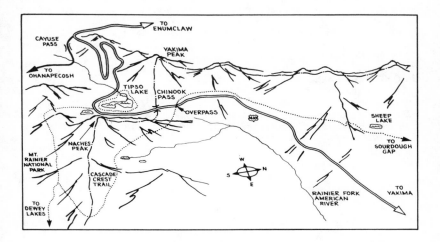

J AMERICAN RIVER

41 MORSE CREEK

Short hikes lead to high views and pretty waterfalls.
Drive east from Chinook Pass on Highway 410. Turn left (north) in 5.8 miles onto
Morse Creek road No. 176.

BEAR GAP

A steep 2-mile hike to high-ridge views down on the Crystal Mountain ski complex.
Drive to the end of Morse Creek road No. 176 (very rough) through the old Gold Hill
mining area. Some cabins and other structures are on private land. Park at horse-
unloading ramp at end of road.
Follow trail up open huckleberry slopes, remembering to take the switchback west
at an unmarked junction. At the top of the gap walk north for views down on
Crystal. 🚶 🚐

GOLD PANNING

Some experts still pan gold in Morse Creek. But none are known to get rich.
Upper reaches of the creek seem most popular. But make certain you are not on
posted private land or someone's posted mining claim.

AMERICAN RIVER

Follow an old road (now a horse trail) to a camping spot on the American River and
then on to Mesatchee Creek Falls, if you've got the time.
Turn south off Highway 410 about 7.5 miles from Chinook Pass onto road No. 1710.
A difficult turn to see as you drive east.
Find the trailhead in about .25 mile. The overgrown roadway-trail drops downhill for
about 1.25 miles to a horse camp before crossing a footbridge over the American
River.
To see Mesatchee Creek Falls continue on the Mesatchee Creek Trail No. 969 past
a junction in another .25 mile. Trail climbs steadily to a view of the waterfall in about
1.25 miles. No trail to the falls.

UNION CREEK FALLS

A sheer tumble of water framed against gray, lichen-covered rock cliffs. A must for
any serious waterfall collector. .25 mile.
Turn left off Highway 410 about 10 miles from Chinook Pass, just before the highway
crosses Union Creek. Watch for Union Creek Trail sign. Trail starts from a small
primitive picnic area at end of spur.

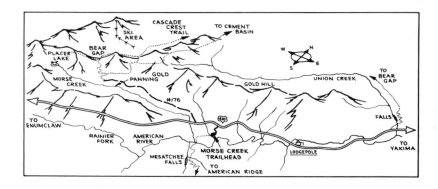

Trail near Bear Gap in Morse Creek Basin

Find falls up a series of switchbacks beyond a log bridge. Two downhill spurs off the main trail lead to best vista points. Trail tends to be cliffy. Not for uncontrolled children. 🚶 🛏

Nearest camping
  Lodgepole, Pleasant Valley

Rimrock Reservoir

42   BUMPING LAKE

Drive up a sparkling river past a soda spring to high vistas and a cross section of mountain lakes.

Drive 20 miles east of Chinook Pass on Highway 410, turning south on the Bumping River road No. 174. Or drive west from the Naches Ranger Station 11.4 miles. End of the river road at Deep Creek Campground, 20 miles.

SODA SPRING

Fluffy pancakes or fizzy pop — soda water for both from a bubbling spring near the Soda Spring Campground.

Cross a wooden bridge at the south end of the campground near the picnic shelter. Follow trail to the left. Springs bubble from rock-walled basins. Drinkable water. Bring your own cup or jug. 🚶 🚗

For other walks go south along the river on fisherman-type trails. Pick your own way. The Bumping River is a talkative stream and well worth listening to.

MINER'S RIDGE

Look out at Mt. Rainier and Mt. Aix and down on the marshy meadows, small lakes, and alpine ponds of the Bumping River drainage.

Drive 2.4 miles up a narrow, twisty road beyond the Granite Lake Campground. 6 miles from Bumping River road No. 174. 14 miles from Highway 410.

Views from a parking area on the edge of the ridge below the site of a former lookout. More private glimpses, however, can be had by walking south along the ridge, framing the scenery as you want it. No trails, just meadows.

LILY LAKE

Follow a series of short trails to two small lakes — one with an island — and views down on a tumbling rapids in the Bumping River.

From the turnoff to the Bumping Lake Campground, drive south on road No. 174 to Deep Creek road No. 162 in 2.3 miles, turning right (west) on Granite Creek road No. 163 keeping right again on road No. 174.

Trail to Fish Trap Lake in 1.8 miles, to Lily Lake in another .3 mile and to the Bumping River in another .8 mile.

Primitive camp spots at both lakes and a small island only a few yards offshore in Lily Lake. You'll need to swim there or else carry in a boat.

Find vistas down on the Bumping River rapids about a half-mile down the Swamp Lake Trail No. 970. From the vista point, the trail drops down to the river — several camping spots nearby.

No bridge. Trail continues on to Swamp Lake in 3 miles.

TWIN LAKES

Hike 2 miles to two of the largest lakes in this part of the proposed Cougar Lakes Wilderness and to the edge of one of the great lake plateaus in the Cascades.

Find the trail out of the Deep Creek Campground at the end of road No. 162, about 7 miles from its junction with No. 174.

Follow trail No. 980 about 1.5 miles to Little Twin Sister Lake and another half-mile to the right (west) to Big Twin Sister Lake. Campsites on both lakes.

If you have the time, camp at the lakes and explore the dozens of unnamed (and unmarked) tarns and smaller lakes nearby. Wild, beautiful country this. And it should be kept that way.

Nearest camping

American Fork, Cedar Springs, Cougar Flats, Bumping Crossing, Bumping Dam, Bumping Lake, Deep Creek, Granite Lake

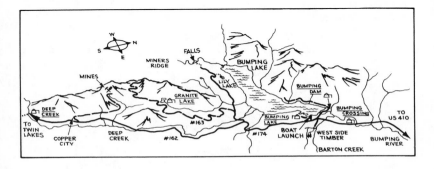

K   THE NACHES

Prowl a cave, skirt waterfalls, and find high vistas.

Drive south from Enumclaw on Highway 410 over Cayuse and Chinook Passes. From Chinook Pass to the Naches Ranger Station through Wenatchee National Forest it's 31.5 miles.

If you seek heat stay in the lowlands below the Little Naches. For cooler temperatures visit the upper valleys and high ridges. Watch for rattlesnakes in lower areas; very few reported above the ranger station.

One warning: This entire area gets heavy motorized use. Four-wheeled vehicles and scooters abound, particularly on summer weekends. However many trails and roads in the area are closed to motorized and horse travel. Such areas are signed. So confine your explorations to them. A list of restricted areas can be obtained at the Naches Ranger Station.

CAMPGROUNDS

Little Naches — 17 sites near the highway at the Little Naches road junction. Heavy trailer use. Pit toilets.

Kaner Flats — 46 units. Picnic area on the river. Quality of campground roads, however, overshadows the rest of the development. Pit toilets. Well water. 2.3 miles from Highway 410 on road No. 197. Fee.

Longmire Meadows — A pretty open meadow often overrun with vehicles. No defined sites. 4 miles on road No. 197 from Highway 410.

Sawmill Flat — 3 tent and 16 trailer sites. Well-defined camp. Pit toilets. Well water. 6.7 miles north of the Naches Ranger Station.

Halfway Flats — 12 sites in a pleasant but poorly defined area. Not as heavily used as some camps. 2.8 miles from Highway 410. Pit toilets. On road No. 175.

Cottonwood — 16 sites in a river-bottom cottonwood brake. Pit toilets. Well water. .7 mile north of ranger station. Fee.

Crow Creek — 16 units in an open flat. Heavy trailer use. 3 miles from highway on road No 182. Pit toilets.

Sand Creek — 6 units. A primitive site in open meadow. Pit toilets. 9 miles from highway on road No. 182.

Huckleberry — 8 units. A primitive site in low brush and open timber. Views of Fife Peaks. Pit toilets.

Clover Spring — 8 sites in subalpine setting. Often overrun with horses or vehicles. Pit toilets. 16.3 miles from junction of road No. 1707 and Highway 410. Excellent view of Mt. Aix and the North Fork of Rattlesnake area.

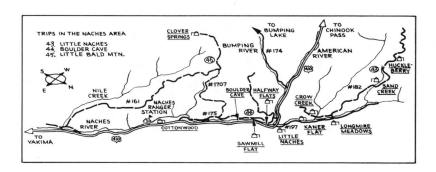

Canyon near Boulder Cave

Naches Wagon Trail near West Fork Bear Creek

43   LITTLE NACHES

Travel an old pioneer trail or drive to Raven Roost for views of all the state's major peaks.

From Seattle, drive south through Enumclaw on Highway 410 to Chinook Pass, continuing another 23.5 miles down the American River to junction with Little Naches road No. 197.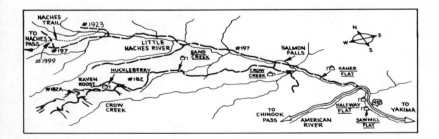

RAVEN ROOST

Adams, Stuart, Baker, Shuksan, Rainier—all in addition to the starring local peak, 7772-foot Mt. Aix.

Drive 13 miles from the Little Naches to a view area near a microwave station. Turn west on road No. 182 about 10.5 miles from Highway 410. A .25-mile spur road, 182-A, near the 13-mile mark leads to the viewpoint at 6191 feet.

One of the best vista points in the Naches Ranger District. The lower road twists through timber before reaching high views the last few miles.

SALMON FALLS

Not as spectacular now as it must have been when salmon battled it, before downstream dams blocked their way. But still worth listening to.

Just south of the Longmire Meadow camping area on Little Naches road No. 197, about 11.5 miles from Highway 410. On the right.

NACHES TRAIL

History tends to get lost here in the grinding dust of the four-wheeled vehicle.

From Little Naches road No. 197 turn right onto road No. 1999, driving a half-mile. Naches Trail on the left. Trail winds 5 miles to Naches Pass.

Early settlers followed the Naches Trail over Naches Pass to Puget Sound. Faced by steep slopes on the west side of the Pass settlers killed stock in order to get hide ropes for lowering wagons downhill.

Nearest camping

Little Naches, Kaner Flat, Longmire Meadow, Crow Creek, Sand Creek, Huckleberry

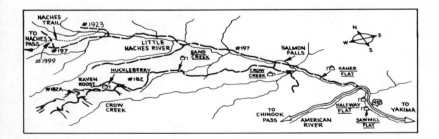

44   BOULDER CAVE

Discover a hidden waterfall before exploring the dark, musty recesses of a 400-foot cavern.

Drive south from Enumclaw on Highway 410 to Chinook Pass. Turn right off Highway 410 about 27 miles from the pass (3.3 miles south of the Little Naches junction), crossing the Cliffdell Bridge and continuing right on road No. 175 to the Boulder Cave Picnic area, 1.2 miles from the highway. 🚗

From the picnic ground follow a heavily used trail uphill. Trail climbs along the side of a canyon before dropping down to the falls and the mouth of the cave in a half-mile.

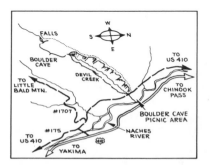

At the bottom of the canyon, cross the creek and climb to the right over rocks upstream to the waterfall tumbling through a gash in the cliff. Mouth of the cave, 200 feet wide and 50 feet high, hangs over Devils Creek like a monstrous hood. The cave was cut by the creek after it was dammed by a slide.

Don't venture into the cave without proper shoes and light. Much of the cavern is dark due to twists and turns. Follow the creek bed to the exit or climb over a ledge outside the cave to see where the stream comes out. Scramble up the side of the canyon to get back to the trail. 🏃

Two warnings: Don't throw anything into the canyon — others may be exploring way trails below you — and watch for rock falling from above.

Boulder Cave

K THE NACHES

45 LITTLE BALD MOUNTAIN

Meadows at 6000 feet, lookout-site views and a lake. But, unfortunately, hordes of trail vehicles on rutted roads that are seldom maintained in what has been converted into an exclusive "wilderness" for four-wheeled vehicles.

No place for anyone looking for peace and quiet.

From Chinook Pass drive west about 27 miles, turning right to cross the Cliffdell Bridge (4.6 miles upriver from the Naches Ranger Station). Turn right again beyond the bridge onto road No. 175 and drive about .25 mile, turning left onto road No. 1707. Junction with Clover Springs road No. 161 in 10.5 miles from the highway.

LITTLE BALD VIEWPOINT

Views of Rainier, Glacier, Stuart, and the Enchantment Peaks from the site of a former lookout tower at 6198 feet. Old Scab Mountain and Mt. Aix hide Adams and St. Helens.

Drive west 2.8 miles from the junction of road No. 1707 with ridge road No. 161, turning north on a lookout spur of less than a half-mile.

An easy point to reach. No steep drives. Best view from the parking area below the tower site.

FLATIRON LAKE

A pleasant lake, shaped as it's named, in open meadows at 5700 feet.

Hike a half-mile by trail from a sign on the west side of road No. 161 about 1 mile north of Clover Spring Campground. The lake lies against the base of the ridge to the south. Trail gets heavy trail bike use.

Best to visit early in the summer before flocks of sheep (every other year) and vehicles (some years) have battered the meadows. And don't add to the trash at the lake. Carry yours back. 🛉

CLOVER SPRING

High meadows, open ridges, and clear vistas — providing you get there before the motorized hordes have whipped much of the landscape into ruts of dust.

Drive to the end of road No. 161 about 5.8 miles from the junction with road No. 1707 from Highway 410. Trails for four-wheeled vehicles continue beyond camp. Don't attempt to follow them in a passenger car.

From the primitive campground climb the slight ridge to the west for views down on the Bumping River valley and Soda Springs Campground, with Rainier and Mt. Adams in the background.

Four-wheeled machines have left their scars everywhere but if you hike out along the lips of the sharp ridges around rock outcrops you can escape some of the mess. 🚍

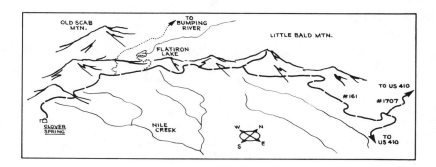

Flatiron Lake

Nearest camping
   Clover Spring, Undeveloped primitive spots in open areas, along the high road, Cottonwood

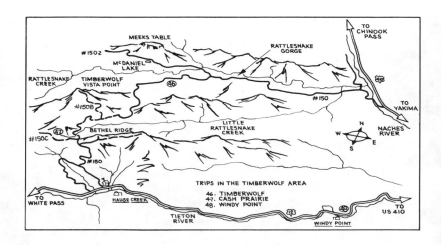

Map labels: TO CHINOOK PASS, MEEKS TABLE, #1502, RATTLESNAKE GORGE, McDANIEL LAKE, RATTLESNAKE CREEK, TIMBERWOLF VISTA POINT, 46, #150B, #150, TO YAKIMA, #150C, BETHEL RIDGE, LITTLE RATTLESNAKE CREEK, NACHES RIVER, #150, N W E S, TO WHITE PASS, HAUSE CREEK, TRIPS IN THE TIMBERWOLF AREA, 46. TIMBERWOLF, 47. CASH PRAIRIE, 48. WINDY POINT, TIETON RIVER, WINDY POINT, TO US 410

L   TIMBERWOLF

A scenic cross-section of Eastern Washington on a high, dry road between the White Pass and Chinook Pass Highways.

Either drive east from Chinook Pass on Highway 410 about 40 miles, turning westerly at the Eagle Rock Scaling Station. Or drive east from White Pass on U.S. 12, turning north on road No. 150, about 17 miles from the pass or about .25 mile west of the Tieton Ranger Station.

46   TIMBERWOLF

A 37.5-mile drive from one valley to the next. Gorges and vistas.

RATTLESNAKE GORGE

Accurately named. But still worth visiting even if all you do is just look into the 1000-foot gorge from the window of a car.

Turn off Highway 410 south of the Naches Ranger Station at the Eagle Rock Scaling Station, keeping left to road No. 150 in about 2.2 miles.

Best views into the teeming hot canyon about 1 mile inside the forest boundary. The gorge looks more like the coulee country of Central Washington than the foothills of the Cascades. No trails. Explore the gorge if you wish. But remember the rattlesnakes.

MEEKS TABLE

A timbered mesa set aside as an ecological reference area.

Best views of the natural area from the Mt. Aix vista point 13.3 miles from Highway 410 on road No. 150, or 16.6 miles from U.S. 12.

Mature ponderosa pine towering over bunchgrass are being preserved in a natural state. No roads. No trails. Hike to the top of the mesa up the open but steep west slope, picking your own path off road No. 1502 beyond McDaniel Lake.

TIMBERWOLF VISTA POINT

Highlight of the cross-country drive from the Naches River to the Tieton River.

From 6391 feet, views of St. Helens, Rainier, the Goat Rocks, Stuart, the Enchantment Peaks, the tip of Glacier, Mt. Aix, and other peaks of the Cascade Crest.

Meeks Table Natural Area in Rattlesnake Creek valley

From Highway 410, drive about 19 miles on road No. 150 to spur road No. 1508. From U.S. 12, drive 10 miles on road No. 150 to the spur. Vista point is about 2.5 miles from turnoff.

The spur road wanders through several open meadows before climbing a final, steep pitch to a large parking area. Rock hunters seek blue agates in road cuts about 1 mile from the vista point. Watch for elk. ⊨

Nearest camping

Hause Creek, Windy Point, Undeveloped primitive camp sites

Bethel Ridge and Mt. Rainier

47 CASH PRAIRIE

The southern half of the trip from the Naches River to Tieton River leads to high viewpoints over Rimrock and Clear Lakes and the Tieton valley.

Turn north off U.S. 12 about 17 miles east of White Pass or about .25 mile west of the Tieton Ranger Station on road No. 150. Or approach the section from the north by turning off Highway 410 8.5 miles below the Naches Ranger Station.

BURNT MOUNTAIN TRAIL

From a heavily-wooded parking loop walk out a ridge trail to open-meadow vistas swinging from Adams to the south past Rainier to Mt. Aix.

Turn east off road No. 150 onto the Cash Prairie road No. 150C about 6.8 miles north of U.S. 12 or 23.1 miles southwest of Highway 410. Road ends in about 2 miles.

Follow the Ironstone Mountain trail west from the parking area, hiking as far as you like. Burnt Mountain in about 2 miles. Open meadows in about 1 mile.

GHOST ROCK OVERLOOK

Look down on the Tieton River valley over pale ghosts carved by winds in outcrops of volcanic rock.

Watch for a parking area on the north side of Cash Prairie road No. 150C just before the road reaches the open meadow and corral area of Cash Prairie. Park and climb the slight ridge to the south. Use care. The slopes are covered with loose rock.

Mt. Adams and the Goat Rocks loom over the ghostly forms. A trail follows the ridge top both east and west for shifting glimpses of the eroded shapes.

HIGH VIEWS

Vistas over the Tieton River valley grow cooler and clearer at every turn.

Drive north from U.S. 12 on road No. 150, turning east on spur road No. 140 in 6 miles (23.9 miles from Highway 410). No. 140 is first road east downhill from the Cash Prairie road junction.

First views from road No. 150 as it climbs out of the valley to the ridge. Views change on every switchback.

Spur road No. 140 to a microwave station affords a more sweeping vista from about 6000 feet. No view from the microwave station. Station road is gated.

Nearest camping
Hause Creek, Windy Point, Undeveloped primitive sites

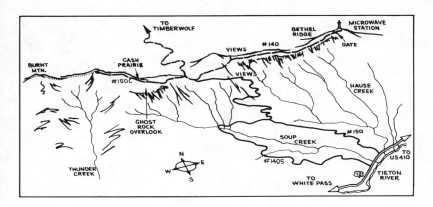

Many-spined prickly pear cactus

48   WINDY POINT

Find desert flowers in valleys and long views from high ridges.

From White Pass drive east on U.S. 12 to the Tieton Ranger Station, about 17 miles. Windy Point Campground 8 miles east of the ranger station and 14 miles west of Naches.

JUMP OFF LOOKOUT

A rough dusty road leads 12 miles — an hour's drive one way — to the edge of Divide Ridge and sweeping views of the Rimrock-Clear Lake basin from 5900 feet.

Turn south off U.S. 12 onto road No. 141 a few hundred yards west of the Windy Point Campground, keeping sharply right at junction at the forest boundary in about 2 miles.

The road, passable in a passenger vehicle if driven carefully, climbs out of the valley to high, open meadows before reaching the manned lookout at the edge of the ridge. Views of the lakes, Rainier, and tip of Adams. No water. 🚙

DESERT FLOWERS

Yellow tissue-paper flowers of the **Prickly Pear Cactus** blossom along roadsides in spring.

Drive east of the Tieton Ranger Station on Highway 12, watching for flowers near the highway, particularly between the game refuge and the junction with Highway 410. 🚙

Flowers bloom in June and early July, growing in prickly clumps of cactus, and by themselves are worth a spring trip into the low-valley country.

Find the rose-colored, ground-hugging **Bitterroot** or Rock Rose on open slopes along the road to Jump Off Lookout. Look for blooms often until late June. 🚙

CAMPGROUND

Windy Point — 8 sites near the highway at 2300 feet. Pit toilets. 14 miles west of Naches. Fee.

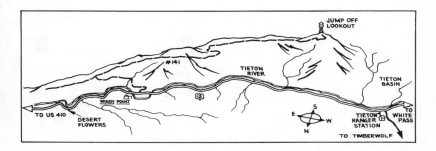

M   THE TIETON

From alpine meadows to desert canyons.

From Enumclaw drive south on Highway 410 to Cayuse Pass, continuing south on Highway 143 to its junction with U.S. 12. About 57 miles from Enumclaw.

Follow U.S. 12 east over White Pass 46 miles to its junction with Highway 410.

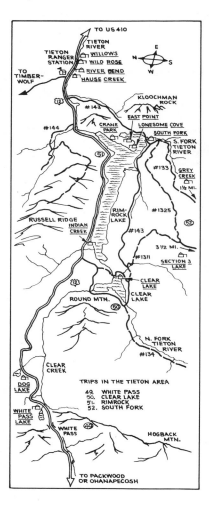

Heavy vehicle use on back roads. Heavy water-skier use on Rimrock Lake. Most trails, though, are posted closed to motorized vehicles.

CAMPGROUNDS

White Pass Lake — 5 camp units on Leech Lake at 4400 feet. Some sites oriented to the lake. Others in timber. Fisherman trails around the north side of the lake. Pit toilets. A half-mile east of White Pass. No motor boats.

Dog Lake — 10 sites in timber area near Dog Lake. Campground on a bench away and above the lake. Primarily a fisherman's camp. 2 miles east of White Pass. Pit toilets.

Indian Creek — 43 units in nicely-developed wooded area just off Rimrock Lake. Some early-summer lake recreation when reservoir is full. Meadows between lake and camp. Heavy holiday use. Piped water. Pit toilets. On U.S. 12 about 8 miles east of White Pass. Fee.

Clear Lake — 64 sites in open timber along east shore of Clear Lake and on Clear Creek. Very few oriented to lake. On road No. 1312. Pit toilets.

Hause Creek — 45 sites on open timbered flat across from the Tieton Ranger Station. Some oriented to the Tieton River. Pit toilets. Piped water. Fee.

River Bend — 5 sites. .25 mile east of Tieton Ranger Station. Pit toilets. Piped water. Fee.

Crane Park — 4 units in uncontrolled area on Rimrock Lake. Drive south on road No. 143, turning off on No. 1431 peninsula loop. Pit toilets.

Lonesome Cove — 4 units near water on peninsula loop road No. 1431. Pit toilets.

East Point — 4 sites in open area near water. An uncontrolled area popular with water-skiers and boaters. On peninsula loop road No. 1431. Pit toilets.

South Fork — 7 sites at mouth of South Fork of Tieton on Rimrock Lake. Turn south off road No.143 just **east** of the bridge over the South Fork. Pit toilets.

Kloochman Rock

Section 3 Lake — A dispersed camp at the end of road No. 1314. No lake. Only a small pollywog pond. Pit toilet. About 11 miles from road No. 143.

Wild Rose — 12 sites, most along the river. Primarily a convoy rest stop on U.S. 12. Heavy trailer use. Pit toilets. Fee.

Willows — 16 sites along the river. A low-altitude area. Trailer use primarily. Pit toilets. Fee.

Grey Creek — 5 sites in wooded area on Grey Creek along the South Fork. Pleasantness of site varies with concentration of motorized equipment. About 5 miles south of Rimrock Lake road No. 143 on road No. 133.

49   WHITE PASS

Leave the "civilization" of ski-lift towers, gas stations, and lodges on trails leading to meadows, forests, and lakes.
From Enumclaw drive south 57 miles to the junction of Highway 143 and U.S. 12. Turn east on 12. White Pass in 12 miles.

DEER LAKE TRAIL
Hike 2 miles across meadows on the Pacific Crest Trail to a small wooded lake at 5206 feet.
Drive to the White Pass Lake Campground on Leech Lake, about .25 mile east of White Pass. Crest Trail starts from the parking area. Look for sign.
The trail climbs north about a half-mile to a junction with one going east to Dog Lake. Keep left. Trail crosses open meadows as it nears the lake.

CASCADE CREST SOUTH
High views and wildflowers from the Pacific Crest Trail south of White Pass.
Take the chairlift at the pass — per-person fee, round trip, packs free — following the Crest Trail south at the top. Walk as far as you like.
Views within 2 miles range from the Goat Rocks around to Rainier. Return to the highway either down a steep trail through timber, or via the chair. Trail continues to Shoe Lake.

CLEAR CREEK FALLS
A 300 foot falls plus high views of the Clear Creek valley with Clear and Rimrock Lakes in the background.
Drive east from White Pass about 2 miles, watching for sign and parking area just east of Dog Lake.
For best views of both the falls and valley, follow a fence about 300 yards down from the parking area. Return via a loop trail through subalpine timber.

Nearest camping
White Pass, Dog Lake, No campgrounds west of the pass on the main highway

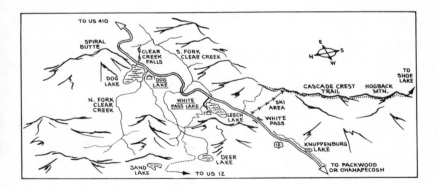

Clear Creek Falls near Dog Lake

M THE TIETON

50 CLEAR LAKE

Climb to a lookout site for views back on two lakes, one chill and clear, the other a reservoir and warm.

Drive east from White Pass on U.S. 12, turning south on road No. 143 about 7 miles from the summit or about 10 miles west of the Tieton Ranger Station.

ROUND MOUNTAIN

Climb 2 miles to view Clear and Rimrock Lakes, Dog Lake, the Tieton River, Spiral Butte, and, of course, the ubiquitous Rainier. Wander the high meadows for the best vistas.

From U.S. 12, drive 3 miles southwesterly on road No. 143 to junction with Round Mountain road No. 130. Find trail at the end of the road in about 4.5 miles at 4200 feet.

Follow a tractor path uphill about .75 mile, picking up an old trail at the topmost part of the track. Watch for a junction 100 yards up the trail; keep right.

In a little more than a mile, after the trail enters open timber, watch for an uphill trail to the left. Lookout site in .25 mile. Take the same route back downhill.

CLEAR LAKE FALLS

A refreshing vista on a hot summer day becomes truly spectacular in winter when the turbulence crystallizes to ice.

Turn off road No. 143 onto road No. 1312 about .75 mile from U.S. 12. Watch for the falls to the right where the road crosses Clear Creek bridge.

The icy water cascades from Clear Lake, plunging over boulders and slabs of rock a half-mile before reaching Rimrock Lake.

SWIMMING

Neither Clear nor Rimrock Lakes offers organized public swimming facilities.

Clear Lake is generally considered too cold for swimming but that doesn't deter everyone. No water-skiers there. Rimrock Lake is pleasant even though the water level may be low in late summer. Simply climb down to the water's edge and plunge.

Most popular swimming spots include Clear Lake Boat Landing, Rimrock Boat Landing, Crane Park Campground, East Point Campground, and Lonesome Cove Campground.

Boaters and water-skiers land at islands in Rimrock Lake to swim from there. Other swimming spots can be seen off road No. 143 on the south side of Rimrock Lake.

Nearest camping

Indian Creek, Clear Lake, Crane Park, Lonesome Cove, East Point

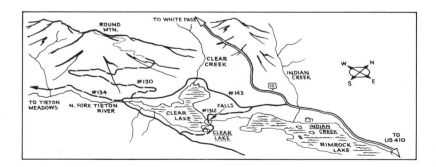

Clear Lake and Rimrock Reservoir from Round Mountain

51   RIMROCK

Basalt columns, soda springs and meadows — all watched over by Kloochman Rock, a volcanic dike which dominates the valley at the lower end of Rimrock Lake.

Drive east from White Pass about 17 miles on U.S. 12 to the Tieton Ranger Station. Turn north on road No. 144 about 2.3 miles west of the station. Turn south on road No. 143 about a half-mile west of the station.

Post piles on road No. 1432

POST PILE

Just as the name implies, a pile of posts. But all of rock. Columnar basalt.

Turn north off U.S. 12 about 2.3 miles west of the Tieton Ranger Station onto Wildcat road No. 144, then again onto road No. 1419. Post Pile in 2.8 miles. Parking areas both above and below the pile.

The basalt core looks as though it started straight up and then curled. Sections of the broken columns are strewn in log-like heaps about the central core. 🚌

RUSSELL RIDGE TRAIL

High views over Rimrock and Clear Lakes with Adams and the Goat Rocks in the background.

Continue past the Post Pile (see above), keeping left onto road No. 1432. Find trail on the west side of the road about .25 mile back from end of the road. Watch for trail sign.

Trail climbs through timber about .75 mile to open slopes with continuous views as far as you want to hike. Walk quietly and watch for elk. 🚶

SODA SPRINGS

A cold soda spring housed in a shelter at a former campground.

Turn east off road No. 143 onto Lost Lake road No. 1402 about .3 mile from U.S. 12 just across the concrete bridge. Turn south sharply onto road No. 1430 within less than another .25 mile.

Watch for a shelter to the west of the road in about 1.5 miles. Find spring inside boggy shelter area. 🚶 🚌

Nearest camping

Hause Creek, East Point, Lonesome Cove, Crane Park

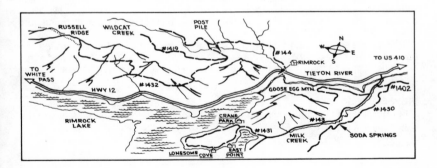

52   SOUTH FORK

A cool waterfall and a high, cool trail — both off dusty roads.
Turn south off U.S. 12 onto the Tieton road No. 143 about a half-mile west of Tieton
Ranger Station. Drive about 4.5 miles, turning south again onto road No. 133.

SOUTH FORK FALLS
A pretty, curved curtain of water filling a rocky canyon with welcome, cooling spray.
Drive about 12 miles on road No. 133 from the lake junction with No. 143 watching
for a wide unmarked parking area on the east side of the road about a mile south of the
Bear Creek bridge.
A zig-zag trail drops about 100 yards or so down a pumice slope to the base of the
falls. Find a cool, misty respite here from the heat of the road. Note the rocks and old
logs crusted with ash from St. Helens.

BLUE SLIDE
Stark ghosts of trees on a river's edge and blue scars on a mountain slope high
above mark a natural catastrophe. All colored now by gray ash from St. Helens.
Drive about 1 mile south of Grey Creek Campground on road No. 133. Or about 8
miles from the junction with road No. 143.
Note gray dead trees on the east side of the river and the blue rock outwash
beneath them. Then look high on the ridge for the notch in rock. The fan of ash and
debris from the slide strangled the trees. ⇥

BEAR CREEK MOUNTAIN TRAIL
Walk through pleasant open meadows at 6500 feet rimmed with subalpine timber
and dotted with wildflowers.
Turn west off road No. 133 onto road No. 1325 about a half-mile from the junction
with No. 143. At the edge of Pinegrass Ridge in 8 miles turn south on road No. 1314,
driving to Section 3 Lake — a frog pond — at the end of the road. Total distance from
No. 143, about 11 miles.
Trail out of a small campground-picnic area at the end of the road winds through one
open meadow after another toward Bear Creek Mountain in 3 miles. Acres and acres
of wildflowers in season. Occasional tarns. Watch for elk from picnic and lunch spots
galore.

VIEW DRIVES
For quick vistas up and down the South Fork of the Tieton River, take any of the
logging spurs off road No. 133. Views on almost every road within a mile or less.

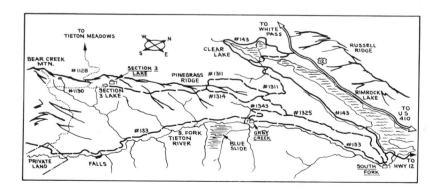

Section 3 Lake

Nearest camping
   South Fork, Grey Creek, Undeveloped primitive spots alongside many of the roads and at Section 3 Lake

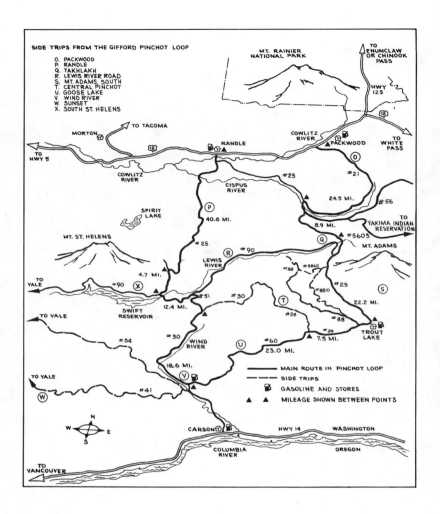

SIDE TRIPS FROM THE GIFFORD PINCHOT LOOP

O. PACKWOOD
P. RANDLE
Q. TAKHLAKH
R. LEWIS RIVER ROAD
S. MT. ADAMS, SOUTH
T. CENTRAL PINCHOT
U. GOOSE LAKE
V. WIND RIVER
W. SUNSET
X. SOUTH ST. HELENS

MT. RAINIER NATIONAL PARK

TO ENUMCLAW OR CHINOOK PASS

HWY 123

TO TACOMA

MORTON

TO HWY 5

COWLITZ RIVER

RANDLE

COWLITZ RIVER

PACKWOOD

TO WHITE PASS

#23

#21

O

CISPUS RIVER

24.5 MI.

#56

SPIRIT LAKE

P

40.6 MI.

8.9 MI.

TO YAKIMA INDIAN RESERVATION

#5603

MT. ST. HELENS

#25

LEWIS RIVER

R

#90

Q

MT. ADAMS

#88

#8860

4.7 MI.

TO YALE

#90

X

#8810

#23

S

#51

#30

T

22.2 MI.

12.4 MI.

SWIFT RESERVOIR

#24

#88

TROUT LAKE

TO YALE

#54

#30

WIND RIVER

U

#60

#24

7.5 MI.

23.0 MI.

18.6 MI.

MAIN ROUTE IN PINCHOT LOOP

TO YALE

#41

V

SIDE TRIPS

GASOLINE AND STORES

W

MILEAGE SHOWN BETWEEN POINTS

N

W   E

S

CARSON

HWY 14   WASHINGTON

COLUMBIA RIVER

OREGON

TO VANCOUVER

140

Indian berry fields and Mt. Adams

N GIFFORD PINCHOT LOOP

Despite the eruption of St. Helens, this part of the state still offers vast recreation opportunities in the huge forest south of Packwood and Randle in a magic triangle watched over by Rainier, Adams and the shell of St. Helens.

Drive south from Enumclaw on Highway 410, continuing over Cayuse Pass to Highway 12, Packwood and Randle.

Although it's only about 160 miles around the major loop from Packwood to Trout Lake to Wind River and back to Randle, never attempt the trip in one day. This is long-weekend and vacation country, strictly. There is too much to see in a day.

And several cautions. If St. Helens is acting up be sure to check on possible forest and road closures before you start. Most of this area has been open since 1981 and will probably remain open. But check at a ranger station before you begin your trip.

If you plan to camp in the middle of the forest (and you most certainly should), watch your gas and food supply. Stores and service stations are found only around the edges of this forest. There are none — NONE — in the middle of it.

O   PACKWOOD

Fresh vistas of Mt. Rainier, high views over the Cowlitz valley, remote campgrounds and crowded ones — all off U.S. 12 and state highway 123.

Drive south from Seattle through Enumclaw, continuing over Cayuse Pass to the lumbering town of Packwood.

CAMPGROUNDS

Ohanapecosh — 229 sites on pleasant timbered loops. Open from mid-May to late October. Often full on a weekend. Evening programs. 1.5 miles south of Stevens Canyon Entrance on state highway 123 in Mt. Rainier National Park. Restrooms. Piped water.

La Wis Wis — 256 units plus a big picnic complex 7 miles north of Packwood. Many sites along the Cowlitz River. Some on Purcell Creek. One of the largest campgrounds in the state. But also the busiest. Heavy reunion use because of its central location. Often crowded. Flush toilets. Piped water.

Summit Creek — 5 sites on a pleasant wooded bench above Summit Creek. About 2 miles from U.S. 12 on road No. 4510. Pit toilets.

Soda Springs — 8 sites in wooded area on loop at the end of road No. 4510, about 5.5 miles from U.S. 12. Not recommended for trailers. Pit toilets.

Walupt Lake — 35 units in the northwest corner of the lake. A relatively open campground. Pit toilets. Boat launching and dock. Views of the Goat Rocks. Piped water.

Walupt Lake Horse Camp — 6 sites near the Walupt Lake Guard Station about 1 mile west of the lake. Fewer mosquitoes but more dusty. Sites are next to road. Good fall camp. Spring water. Pit toilets.

Chambers Lake — A new 15-site campground without any facilities. No water. No toilets. Near the lake.

Packwood and Mt. Rainier in the moonlight

Grove of the Patriarchs

53   OHANAPECOSH

Quiet timbered trails, a rock-framed waterfall, and hot mineral springs — all just a short hike away.

From Enumclaw drive south on Highway 410 to Cayuse Pass, continuing south 11 miles to the Stevens Canyon Entrance Station and another 1.8 miles to Ohanapecosh Campground, both to the right.

SILVER FALLS

Take an easy 3-mile loop walk from the Ohanapecosh Campground or drop .3 mile from the main highway to a noisy, gorge-cased torrent on the Ohanapecosh River.

Find the trail at the end of the bridge on the amphitheater side or off the upper end of the older campground loop behind the Visitor Center. Trail travels above the river to a log bridge below the pretty falls and then winds back on the other side of the stream, ending either near the amphitheater or behind the Visitor Center.

(To hike from the highway, watch for trail sign on the left about .3 mile south of the Stevens Canyon Entrance and about 300 feet north of bridge over Laughingwater Creek. Park beyond the sign on the right.) 🚶

Visit the falls too by hiking south along the river from the entrance station area (trail begins across the road from restrooms). Hike 2 miles past the falls to the campground. 🚶

GROVE OF PATRIARCHS

See trees, some 1000 years old, along an easy 1.5-mile loop trail from the Stevens Canyon Entrance Station area.

Find the trail to the right (north) beyond the entrance station near the restrooms across the Ohanapecosh River.

The level trail crosses the river (take fork right in about a half-mile) to loop around a richly-timbered island in the river. Towering old-growth Douglas fir, hemlock, and cedar.

The largest cedar measures 25 feet in circumference. One Douglas fir measures 38 feet around. 🚶

OHANAPECOSH HOT SPRINGS

What man once altered, time now painfully restores. A recuperating area which illustrates nature's ability to out-wait man.

Take the trail toward Silver Falls from the campground loop behind the Visitor Center, following a nature trail uphill, to a point where soda water bubbles out of the ground. Most of the springs were once capped and confined to bathing tanks.

The Park Service acquired the resort in 1965. All buildings have been removed and the area has been allowed to rejuvenate. 🚶

Nearest camping
Ohanapecosh, La Wis Wis

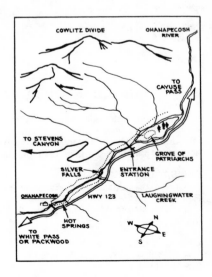

Palisades overlook

54 AYANCE CANYON-SUMMIT CREEK

Viewpoints, waterfalls, a soda spring and trails near White Pass.
From Seattle, drive south from Enumclaw to Cayuse Pass on Highway 410, continuing south on Highway 123 to junction with U.S. 12 to White Pass. Find road No. 4510 about one mile east of the junction off U.S. 12.

PALISADES OVERLOOK
A formal overlook and picnic area with views of columnar basalt palisades and Mt. Rainier.
Drive **west** from White Pass about 10 miles to marked road spur on the south side of the highway. 🚗

LAVA CREEK FALLS
A distant view of a veil of water pluming over lava cliffs into the Clear Fork of the Cowlitz River.
Drive west from White Pass about 7.5 miles to a marked viewpoint on the south side of the highway. No trails to the falls. 🚗

LOGGING ROAD VIEWS

Two logging roads lead to high views of Mt. Rainier and the Goat Rocks.

For views from road No. 1276 turn left (north) off U.S. 12 to White Pass a few hundred feet east of the Palisades Overlook (see above). Follow road No. 1276 about 1.5 miles to a junction with a spur No. 011, to the right. Drive to end of the spur in 3 miles.

For views from road No. 1284, turn north of U.S. 12 about .8 mile **west** of the White Pass Summit. View point in 2.9 miles.

SUMMIT CREEK TRAIL

A pleasant walk through timber past several refreshing streams.

Find trail in the northeast corner of Soda Spring Campground at the end of road No. 4510 about 5.5 miles from U.S. 12. Sign indicates Jug Lake and others.

Trail climbs steadily but easily through timber well away from Summit Creek. Wild flowers, deer, squirrels, sometimes elk, and small streams make the walk more worthwhile than just sitting in a car.

SODA SPRING

A busy bubbling soda spring, one of the fastest running in the region.

Watch for a sign pointing to spring on south side of road No. 4510 just before the road ends at the campground.

The short trail leads to a rolling rock-ringed basin. Like most mountain mineral springs, the water's good — if you like it.

COAL MINE

Scars of the coal-mining operation aren't as obvious as those of the timber "mining" effort.

On road No. 4510 about 4 miles from U.S. 12. The overgrown site gets harder and harder to find.

The forest road cuts across a mining area about .25 mile west of Soda Spring Campground. The boundary is marked obviously by logging on both sides of the road. Watch for coal piles on the south side of the road. A tunnel still exists. But it's dangerous.

Nearest camping

Summit Creek, Soda Springs, White Pass Lake, Dog Lake

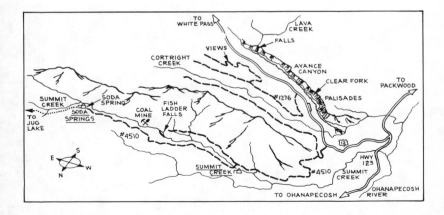

55   LA WIS WIS

Oft-crowded campgrounds but less crowded on trails to falls, pools, and on view roads.

Drive 57 miles south of Enumclaw to the junction with U.S. 12, continuing south another half-mile to the La Wis Wis Campground turnoff to the west.

(There used to be lots of beautiful big trees in this campground which made it one of the most attractive in the state. However, after a falling tree killed a camper in Oregon, the Forest Service logged 196 of the biggest "decadent" trees, collecting $86,000 in the process.)

The Forest Service plans to inaugurate a long-term program to regenerate spots which have been damaged by heavy use. Help preserve the new growth.

Packwood and Mt. Rainier from road No. 48

LA WIS WIS TRAILS

The Ohanapecosh River and Clear Fork join to form the Cowlitz River in the upper end of the campground. Trails follow all three. But the favorite wends south along the Cowlitz across from camp.

Cross a suspension bridge in the campground, taking a well-used trail downstream. The path follows the river (watch for blazes) before climbing the side of a steep slope for views down into the lower end of camp. Not a good trail for uncontrolled children. Trail ends at a logging road in about 1.25 miles. Hike back on the trail. (The bridge, out in 1982, was scheduled for reconstruction in 1983.)

PURCELL FALLS

Four small cascades tumble through a series of fern-draped rock pockets.

Drive through La Wis Wis Campground, keeping to the right at the first campground-loop junction. Sign indicates falls on far side of loop.

Walk about 100 yards to the first small falls. Others higher on the slope. Torrents run busiest in the spring. Stream goes underground below the falls.

BLUE HOLE

A reminder here of the subtle way that man's "improvements" often destroy.

Turn north off the entrance road to La Wis Wis Campground just east of the Guard Station. Walk the spur across the Clear Fork bridge.

Find the pool 30 to 50 yards upstream at a point where the trail starts to climb around a rock bluff. The river forms the Blue Hole where cliffs pinch it together.

The tragedy lies in what's no longer seen. Huge salmon used to crowd the pool each autumn on their upstream runs from the ocean. But no more. Tacoma's downstream Mossyrock Dam blocked the run in 1967.

VIEW DRIVES

Almost every logging road east off U.S. 12 leads to high views of the Packwood valley and Mt. Rainier.

On **Lava Creek** road No. 46, views in 1.5 miles.

On **Purcell Creek** road No. 4610, views in 1 mile.

On road to **Packwood Lake** trail (turn east just south of the Packwood Ranger Station), views from standpipe and from parking area at road end.

On **Hager Creek** road No. 48 (turn off U.S. 12 onto Johnson Creek road No. 21, then onto No. 48), views off second switchback in about 2 miles.

Nearest camping

La Wis Wis

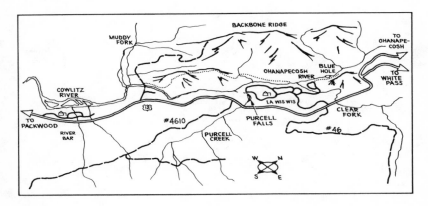

56   GOAT ROCKS

A panoramic preview of the Goat Rocks with glimpses of Mt. Adams tossed in from a forest road that loops south from Packwood and then west to Randle.

Turn left off U.S. 12 onto Johnson Creek road No. 21 about 3 miles south of Packwood. After a series of switchbacks the road sweeps south toward Chambers and Walupt Lakes before turning westward to join road No. 23, leading to Randle and U.S. 12 again in about 49 miles.

Best views of the mountains between the Johnson Creek and Chambers Creek drainages.

WALUPT CREEK TRAIL

Hike 2 miles to open flower meadows with views back down on Walupt Lake.

Turn east off road No. 21 onto road No. 2160 to Walupt Lake. Turnoff is about 16.5 miles from U.S. 12 south of Packwood or about 33 miles from Randle. Campground (follow Walupt Lake signs) in about 4.5 miles.

Hike east out of the Walupt Lake Campground on trail along the north side of the lake. Trail reaches the first of a series of open meadows after crossing Walupt Creek in about 2 miles. Pacific Crest Trail in another 2 miles.

CHAMBERS LAKE

A small mountain lake tucked in timber at the foot of the Goat Rocks.

Turn off Johnson Creek Road No. 21 onto road No. 2150 about 13.5 miles from U.S. 12, south of Packwood. Lake in about 4 miles.

Improvements have been promised in this heavily-used area for years. But the Forest Service continues to plead lack of funds. No toilet facilities, for instance, have been installed because the agency contends it cannot afford to put them in or service them. When you visit here, then, note the heavy logging and wonder about the agencies' lack of money.

NANNIE RIDGE TRAIL

It's 3.5 miles to the top of Nannie Peak, but a 2-mile hike will take you into light

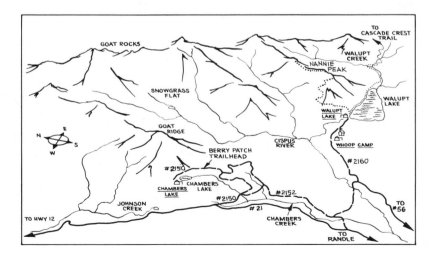

Walupt Lake and Lakeview Mountain

timber with views out toward Walupt Lake and the rest of the glories in this high country.

Start out on the Walupt Creek Trail (see above) turning uphill onto the Nannie Ridge Trail in a few yards. The first 1.5 miles in timber. Views at about 2 miles.

If you continue another mile, the trail tops the ridge. Add a half-mile hike up an unmarked way trail to reach a former lookout site atop Nannie Peak at 5800 feet.

Nearest camping
   Walupt Lake, Whoop Camp, Chambers Lake

P   RANDLE

Big mountains, high meadows, private waterfalls, lakes, a pretty gorge and lots of huckleberries — all off roads both north and south of Randle, headquarters of the Randle District of the Gifford Pinchot National Forest.

Drive south from Enumclaw on Highway 410, continuing over Cayuse Pass to U.S. 12. Randle lies 25 miles south of the White Pass Highway junction on U.S. 12. Ranger station at the east end of town, as you come in, on the left. (Drive to Randle also via Morton. Same distance and quicker. But not as scenic.)

CAMPGROUNDS

Tower Rock — 15 units on Cispus River. Most sites oriented to river. A damp cottonwood-and-cedar area. Piped water. Pit toilets.

North Fork — 31 units on the south side of the North Fork of the Cispus River off road No. 23. Guard station. Piped water. Pit toilets. Fee.

Blue Lake Creek — 9 units, developed by the Job Corps, in a hardwood glade surrounded by grass meadows. Pit toilets. Trail down Blue Creek to Cispus River.

Adams Fork — 23 units in park-like stand of fir. Sites back from the Cispus River. Pumped water. Pit toilets.

Cat Creek — 6 sites near Cat Creek. A small camp in a heavily-used but primitive area. Pit toilets.

Pole Patch — 12 units in thin, subalpine timber at 4400 feet. Views of all three major peaks from ridge just above camp. Light use except during huckleberry season. Piped water. Pit toilets.

Iron Creek — 54 units. A very pleasant camp in lovely timber stand. Some sites on Iron Creek. Others above the Cispus River. Many on loops. Piped water. Fee.

Burley Mountain road

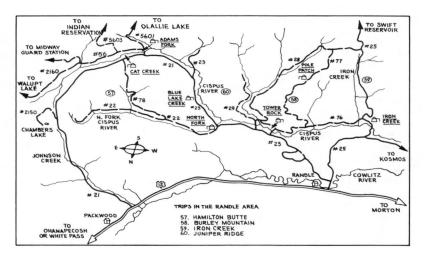

TO INDIAN RESERVATION
TO OLALLIE LAKE
TO SWIFT RESERVOIR
TO MIDWAY GUARD STATION
#5603
#5601
ADAMS FORK
#56
#25
#2160
#21
#23
#28
POLE PATCH
#77
IRON CREEK
TO WALUPT LAKE
CAT CREEK
CISPUS RIVER
60
59
#2150
57
BLUE LAKE CREEK
58
#22
#78
#23
#29
TOWER ROCK
N. FORK CISPUS RIVER
#22
NORTH FORK
#76
IRON CREEK
CHAMBERS LAKE
CISPUS RIVER
#23
#25
JOHNSON CREEK
TO KOSMOS
RANDLE
COWLITZ RIVER
12
TO MORTON
#21
PACKWOOD
TRIPS IN THE RANDLE AREA
57. HAMILTON BUTTE
58. BURLEY MOUNTAIN
59. IRON CREEK
60. JUNIPER RIDGE
TO OHANAPECOSH OR WHITE PASS

Yozoo Creek Falls on road No. 78

57 HAMILTON BUTTE

High views, waterfalls, and pretty lakes, all surrounding a single mountain.
Turn south (left) off U.S. 12 at the main intersection in Randle crossing the Cowlitz River. At the first junction in about 1 mile turn left onto road No. 23. Turn left off 23 onto road No. 22, the North Fork road, in about 11.5 miles from Randle.

HAMILTON BUTTE VIEW
Spend an hour, an afternoon, or lug a pack and spend the night on high, clear meadows close to the stars. A 1-mile hike.
Turn right off the North Fork road No. 22 onto road No. 78 about 5.8 miles from the junction with No. 23. Follow No. 78 about 7.5 miles turning left (eastward) toward Mud Lake onto road No. 7807.
At Mud Lake turn right, following a spur road no farther than a mile-post marker. Park and climb to the trailhead in about .25 mile.
Modest views mostly to the south on the way up the trail. Best views are reserved for those who complete the short climb.

Rainier, St. Helens, Adams, Hood with the Goat Rocks lined up like soldiers to the east. And all of them above meadows colored with purple penstemon and sego lilies.

To drive back, continue east on road No. 7807 as it winds through an old burn before dropping down to road No. 21. Or return to road No. 78, turn left and drive down to the Cat Creek Guard Station, also on No. 78.

YOZOO AND GROUSE CREEK FALLS

Fragile, park-size spectacles tucked away near over-awing roads. Best in early summer.

Turn right off road No. 22 onto road No. 78. Yozoo Creek in about 4 miles. Grouse Creek in another 1 mile. Watch for both falls where the road turns toward the mountain.

Yozoo Creek Falls — A pretty zig-zag of water slipping across mossy rock slabs in a shaded tunnel of trees.

Grouse Creek Falls — A sparkling stairstep cascade ending in a glistening spread over a slab of rock.

WOBBLY LAKE

A modest lake nowhere near as revolutionary as its name, once given members of the International Workers of the World. 1.75 miles.

Turn right off road No. 22 onto road No. 2208 about 8.3 miles from the junction with No. 23. Watch for Wobbly Lake trail sign in about 2.8 miles.

Trail climbs easily to a small open lake at 3400 feet. The lake, below Hamilton Butte and Elk Peak, lies in an open old burn. Huckleberries in autumn. 3 tables and pit toilet.

Reach the lake also from road No. 7807 beyond Mud Lake. Watch for sign. This steeper trail drops down to the lake in about 1.5 miles.

Nearest camping
North Fork, Cat Creek, Adams Fork

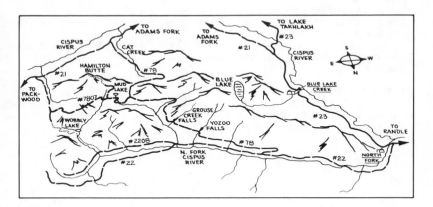

58   BURLEY MOUNTAIN

A colorful huckleberry-ridge drive watched over by all three sentinel peaks of the southern Washington Cascades.

Drive south from Randle on either road No. 23 or 25, turning off at junctions with road No. 76. Turnoff to Burley Mountain road No. 77 in 4.4 miles from Iron Creek Campground and 2.4 miles from Tower Rock Campground.

The narrow dirt road climbs through forest to high ridges just below Burley Mountain, continuing south to Mosquito Meadows and road No. 28 in about 18 miles. Continue across No. 28 on road No. 2816 to reach Badger Peak Trail.

Return to road No. 76 either by turning left onto road No. 28 or right toward the Randle-Lewis River road No. 25.

Rainier, Adams, and St. Helens peer down on the narrow ridge road one after the other as it winds back and forth across the crest, with all three showing up at once on some of the turns.

The ridge is seldom busy in midsummer. But during the huckleberry season up to 1000 people have been counted in the area. The narrow, steep roads are not recommended for trailers. ⌐🚐

BURLEY MOUNTAIN

360 degrees of grandeur, sweeping from Hood through Adams, St. Helens, Rainier, the Goat Rocks and back to the top of Hood — with rolling ridges in between.

Turn off the Burley Mountain road No. 77 (see above) about 7.6 miles from the valley junction with road No. 76. Follow the narrow spur (No. 7605), penciled onto the side of the mountain all the way to a lookout site, or park at the junction and walk the 1.5 miles. ⌐🚐

Slopes around the mountain abound with huckleberries.

PINTO ROCK

A towering backbone of rock eroded and etched by the wind and weather.

Drive south on road No. 77 about 8 miles beyond the lookout turnoff. The rock looms over the road to the left. ⌐🚐

Park in a saddle just south of the outcrop if you want to explore. Top of the outcrop, 5113 feet. But don't attempt to climb it unless you are both skilled and equipped. Very loose rock.

BADGER PEAK

Drive, then hike 1.5 miles across ash-blanketed slopes to an old lookout site with views into the maw of St. Helens and out at Adams and Rainier.

If you're driving south from Burley Mountain on road No. 77, jog east a few hundred

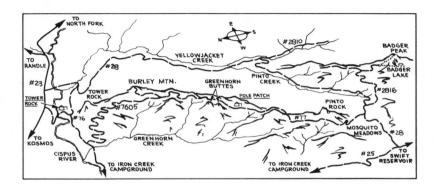

Juniper Peak from Burley Mountain

yards at Mosquito Meadows on road No. 28 and then right (south again) another 4.5 miles on No. 2816 to the end of the road.

From the Cispus Center follow road No. 28 up Yellowjacket Creek turning left (south) at Mosquito Meadows onto road No. 2816.

Find the trail around the side of the ridge to the right. It was drifted with ash from St. Helens. At the saddle, follow the trail south (left) to the old lookout site at 5664 feet.

Badger Lake lies only a half-mile from the lookout but some 1600 feet below it.

TOWER ROCK

A 3337-foot tower of rock spires above the Cispus River valley.

Best views of the rock from road No. 76 south of Tower Rock Campground. No trails. For skilled rock climbers only.

Some people say they can see the form of an Indian stretched out on the side of the tower near the top. Others don't see it at all.

Nearest camping

Tower Rock, Pole Patch, North Fork, Iron Creek

59   IRON CREEK

Turn south off Highway 14 in Randle, crossing the Cowlitz River and then continuing south, following Randle-Lewis River road markers. Iron Creek Campground, just across the Cispus River, in about 9.7 miles. Junction with road No. 28 leading to

Quartz Creek Big Tree Area

Mosquito Meadows, Badger Mountain, and back to Tower Rock area in about 12.6 miles from the campground junction.

IRON CREEK CAMPGROUND TRAILS

Hike along the Cispus River and up Iron Creek on trails around the outer rim of Iron Creek Campground.

Find trails near the river and creek from any of the sites in this pleasant, timbered area.

A 1-mile hike takes you along both creeks. Return to your campsite via cross-camp trails.

IRON CREEK FALLS

Iron Creek shoots over a cliff into a pool just below the road.

Drive about 10 miles south of Iron Creek Campground on road No. 25. Waterfall is on the left (east) side of the road about halfway between junctions of roads No. 2517 and No. 99.

Best view from a curve high above the creek where the road turns toward the creek (going south) or away from the creek (going north). No trails. But some have scrambled down a steep bank for better views.

QUARTZ CREEK BIG TREE AREA

62 acres of prime Douglas fir, some 7 feet in diameter and 250 feet tall, in a botanical preserve.

From Iron Creek Campground drive northwest on road No. 25 to road No. 26, the Ryan Lake road. Drive southerly on No. 26 onto road No. 2608 in about 9 miles.

Grove lies in a swampy area between the first and second clearcuts on No. 2608. No trails. But an old bulldozer track leads partway into the grove near the second clearcut, on the left.

RYAN LAKE

A pretty lake — before St. Helens did its thing — but a shambles now.

Worth a trip just to see the damage caused by the volcanic blast and also the nature and extent of salvage logging. Remember, as you look, that much of this area had already been logged before the blast and that much of the debris you see resulted from that.

Either drive in and out on road No. 26 or else continue south on No. 26 to Meta Lake, looping back on road No. 99 to No. 25. (See Spirit Lake, page 214.)

Nearest camping
Iron Creek

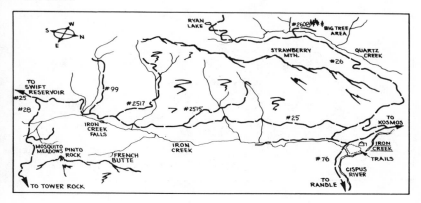

P   RANDLE

60   JUNIPER RIDGE

Two mountains on a single ridge with different trails and vistas.

Walk through forest to reach one peak with a straight-down view (or so it seems) into the Cispus River. Hike through enchanting meadows to the other with entrancing views of distant peaks.

TONGUE MOUNTAIN

All of the interesting surprises on this 2-mile hike are left for the very end.

To find the trail, turn off road No. 23 (to Trout Lake) onto road No. 28 (watch for the Cispus Environmental Center signs) and then left onto road No. 29 in a little more than a mile.

From road No. 29, turn left on road No. 2904 in about 4 miles. Find the Tongue Mountain Trail at the top of a pass in another 4 miles.

Take the trail north from the pass and climb through scraggly forest for about 1.25 miles to reach an unmarked trail to the right (uphill) just as the main trail starts generally downward.

The path to the mountain top climbs quickly to open meadows — lots of flowers in season — and then zig-zags gracefully, safely and persistently uphill across open slopes to a cleft between two rock peaks. (The path here, although not heavily used, is fairly well marked by fresh St. Helens pumice.)

Don't rush the last few feet. The trail ends abruptly at the edge of a cliff with a breathtaking drop of 3200 feet to the Cispus River.

Big views of St. Helens, Rainier and Adams from the cleft. Follow faint way trails up through the rocks to the top.

SUNRISE PEAK

Easy alpine meadows here. But find the greatest spectacle from the lookout site at 5892 feet.

Drive toward Trout Lake on road No. 23 (see above) turning right (east) onto road No. 2324 about 5 miles beyond the Walupt Lake junction. Find the trailhead in another 5 miles on the left at what looks like an uphill logging spur.

The path starts on the abandoned logging road and then climbs quickly and sharply to meadows in about a half-mile. Views here of Rainier, Adams and Hood.

From now on take your pick. Follow the trail across huckleberry meadows toward Jumbo Peak to the southwest. You can't get lost. Lots of flowers in early summer and lots of huckleberries in the fall.

Or make your way uphill to views from Sunrise Peak. Two approaches even here. Take a sometimes-signed and always-faint trail uphill to the right about .25 mile after

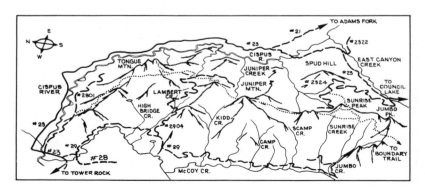

Tongue Mountain trail

you crest the meadow plateau. The trail climbs sharply on a long traverse to a series of switchbacks up the west side of the peak.

Or follow the meadow trail straight ahead to the first saddle. Turn right here and follow a trail uphill to a higher saddle on the north side of the mountain. Lots of vistas here: Rainier, Adams along with St. Helens' gaping crater.

To go on to the peak from this saddle find a faint rut (not quite a trail) through trees uphill to the south, joining the switchbacks in about .25 mile.

Climb to the lookout site atop rocks — with care. Or enjoy easier vistas from a ledge where the trail ends.

Q   TAKHLAKH

This high plateau — all of it above 4000 feet — defines itself. Other terms from other places will not fit at all. Suffice to say, simply, that once visited it demands your return again.

At Randle, turn left (south) off U.S. 12 onto the Trout Lake-Randle road at the town's only major intersection. Follow road No. 23 to Baby Shoe Pass in 33 miles, turning left onto road No. 2329 for Takhlakh Lake, Olallie Lake, and Midway.

Continue on No. 23 — avoiding turn-off to the Trout Lake end of the Randle-Trout Lake road — for Council Lake.

CAMPGROUNDS

Takhlakh Lake — 42 units in sparsely-timbered area near lake, all with views of Mt. Adams. Boat ramp. Swimming. Pit toilets. Fee.

Olallie Lake — 5 sites in open area near lake. Some sites with views of Adams. Trail around lake. Pit toilets.

Council Lake — 11 units on pleasant timbered bench above the lake. Lake too cold for swimming. Pit toilets. Fee.

Killen Creek — 8 units along a single spur road. Near creek. Some sites with view of Adams. Pit toilets.

Horseshoe Lake — 10 units in timber area. Most sites away from the lake. A fisherman's camp. Boat launching. Pit toilets.

Spring Creek — 3 units in heavy-wooded area. Some sites near small creek. No views. Glimpses of Rainier to the north through trees on the access road. Pit toilets.

Midway — Primitive camping west of the site of the guard station on road No. 2329. 4 tables. Views as you find them. Pit toilets.

Chain of Lakes — 3 sites near the shore of a lake at the end of spur road No. 022 from road No. 5601 to Olallie Lake.

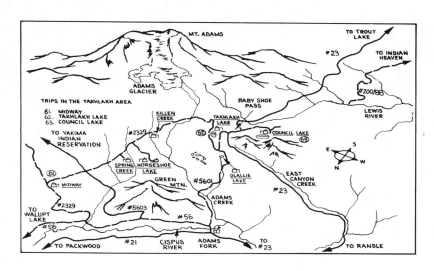

Q TAKHLAKH

61 MIDWAY

In autumn, miles of glistening scarlet below the snow-heaped north side of Mt. Adams.

Turn left off the Trout Lake-Randle road (No. 23) onto road No. 2329 at Baby Shoe Pass and right in less than a mile, following No. 2329 past Takhlakh Lake. Midway, site of a guard station, 10.6 miles from the pass junction. Or from Packwood, take Johnson Creek road No. 21, turning first onto Walupt Lake road No. 2160 and then right onto No. 656. Turn left on road No. 2329 in about 25 miles to reach Midway.

MIDWAY VIEW

Climb atop huge boulders to look over the huckleberry meadows of Mt. Adams with Hood, St. Helens and Rainier added for free. Note Potato Hill, the little volcano to the south.

Drive east past the Midway junction to a "road closed" sign on the left and then walk north about 2 miles on the abandoned road to a tumble of rocks and a 360-degree vista.

Note, as you walk through the open meadows, that the "road closed" sign has been totally ignored by off-road vehicles which have avoided the sign by driving up the Pacific Crest Trail. Wonder, again, about Forest Service management foresight in "closing" a road which has really remained open to many. ⚡

MIDWAY MEADOWS

Skies loaded with stars, fresh air without bound, meadows, and mountains — let each camper mix his own.

Either west or south of the Midway junction, find your own meadow, your own view, and your own corner of sky or mountain. Best in the fall. Mosquitoes are fewer then and huckleberries turn the whole scene into an unbelievable explosion of red.

If you camp outside an established camping area be careful not only of fire (these meadows get tinder-dry) but of trash. The beauty of this country can only survive the impact of men if men have the thoughtfulness to remember tomorrow. 🚶 🚗

MUDDY MEADOWS

Soggy wildflower meadows stretched below towering Mt. Adams with white-hatted Rainier and St. Helens standing guard to the north and west.

Turn east (toward Mt. Adams) onto road No. 087 just south of the Spring Campground turnoff. 3.2 miles south of Midway junction. Road ends at a primitive camping spot in 1 mile.

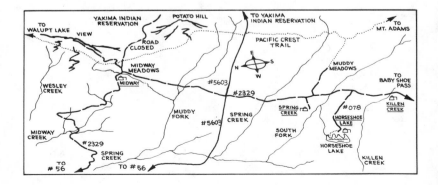

Horseshoe Lake and Mt. Adams

Either follow a trail toward the mountain (Pacific Crest Trail junction in 1.5 miles) or make your own way in almost any direction over meadows full of color and mountains. Trail eastward climbs into light timber in about 1 mile. All sorts of bog-oriented wildflowers in season.

HORSESHOE LAKE
Walk out on any of the several peninsulas along the campground side of the lake for surprise views of a watchful Adams.

Turn away from the mountain (west) onto Horseshoe Lake spur about 3.9 miles south of Midway.

Hike fisherman trails to peninsulas both ways from the campground. Or better yet, prowl the lake by canoe. Motor speed limited by regulation.

The lake was created by CCC crews in the 1930s when they dammed a meadow stream. Beaver since have added about 3 feet of new dam to the structure, almost completely covering the old dam.

Nearest camping
Spring Creek, Horseshoe Lake, Killen Creek, Primitive sites on meadows to the east.

Q   TAKHLAKH

62   TAKHLAKH LAKE

Start with a lake reflected full of Mt. Adams, then add strange lava heaps and a cluster of 13 smaller lakes.
Turn left off the Trout Lake-Randle road No. 23 onto road No. 2329 at Baby Shoe Pass, following No. 2329 to Takhlakh Lake turnoff in about 1.6 miles.

Takhlakh Lake

TAKHLAKH LAKE TRAIL

If you ever tire of Mt. Adams' big reflection in the lake, take a short, pleasant hike through the woods.

Find trail along the shore of the lake to right from the campground. Less than 1 mile.

A cool quiet forest walk through shady timber. For other diversions, canoe around the shores with Mt. Adams almost in constant view. Swimming too. Refreshing but not paralyzing.

And don't miss the sunsets, with Adams glowing almost every hue above its reflection in the lake. 🚶

CHAIN OF LAKES

Explore 13 lakes on a 50-acre subalpine plateau either on foot or by canoe.

Turn left onto road No. 2329 as you leave the Takhlakh Campground road. Spur road to Chain of Lakes to the right (north) in about a half-mile. Road ends at a campground in boggy meadows in 1 mile.

Most lakes lie north of the road. No formal trails. Find your own way. Some of the lakes are linked by shallow channels. Canoe from one to the other. No motors allowed. Again, to avoid being overwhelmed by mosquitoes, visit in the autumn. 🛶

TAKH TAKH MEADOWS

Spell them anyway you want (maps and signs range from Tack Tack through Tach Tach, Takk Takk, to Takhlakh) but the strange beauty of the meadows remains the same.

Watch for sign (Takh Takh) on the left (north) side of road No. 2329 a little more than 1 mile south of the Takhlakh Campground turnoff. (Turn right as you leave the campground spur.)

Beyond meadows filled with bear grass, lupine, gentians, bog orchids, and other flowers in season, explore huge furrowed piles of black volcanic rock. The heap is among several to be explored in the unmapped area north of the road. Find your own way from one ridge to the next. No trails. Reason for the black piles is not apparent. But the mystery is beautiful, nonetheless.

The name for the meadows apparently came from the Chinook Indian name for the wild camas plant — Takh — which Indians harvested in the meadows.

Nearest camping

Takhlakh Lake, Council Lake, Olallie Lake, Killen Creek

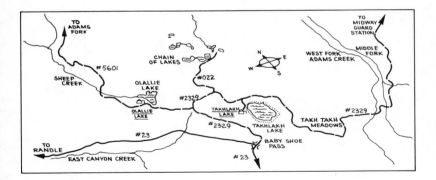

63 COUNCIL LAKE

A single mountain lake with two spectacular nearby viewpoints. Rocks and beaver dams also nearby.

Drive to Baby Shoe Pass on Trout Lake-Randle road (No. 23). Council Lake turnoff in about 1 mile. **Watch signs carefully.**

COUNCIL BLUFF TRAIL

Hike a sharp 1.5 miles to a 360 degree view of everything!

To reach an old lookout site atop the bluff, hike up a closed road at the end of the Council Lake Campground, continuing on a trail as the road ends.

Trail climbs sharply but you can make it easier by avoiding shortcuts beaten out by enthusiastic but unthinking hikers. ↑

BABY SHOE OVERLOOK

Drive about 1 mile across open huckleberry slopes to views westward over Council Lake and toward all the big peaks too.

Turn off the Trout Lake-Randle road (No. 23) less than .25 mile beyond turnoff to Takhlakh Lake-Midway (road No. 2329). Watch for sign on right, road No. 335, keeping left.

Parking at the end of the road in a prime huckleberry area. Views of Adams, St.Helens, Rainier, Hood, and the Goat Rocks. ⟶

ROCKS

Petrified wood, agates, and jasper in road cuts and creek beds near Baby Shoe Pass.

Petrified wood — Road-construction crews found petrified wood in new road cuts near Baby Shoe Pass on the Trout Lake-Randle road (No. 23). No marked areas. Seek your own.

Jasper-Agates — Rockhounds seek both along East Canyon Creek west of the pass on road No. 23. Dark Creek, 8 miles west of the pass, is also a popular rock-hunting area.

BEAVER

Small ponds in shallow meadows — all the work of beaver.

Watch to the left of the road (east) at Baby Shoe Pass. Ponds lie below the road as it heads south. No trails. Prowl the ponds as you will. Binocular views from the road sometimes reveal a beaver or two — if you're lucky.

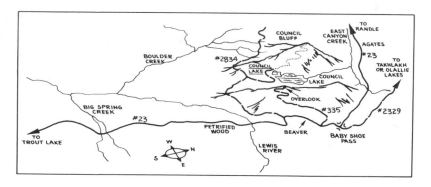

Council Lake and Mt. Adams from Council Bluff

Nearest camping
   Council Lake, Takhlakh Lake, Olallie Lake, Killen Creek

R   LEWIS RIVER ROAD

This fancy new highway, built to trans-state standards, thrusts like a spear from Swift Reservoir into the very heart of the fragile and tender high country west of Mount Adams.

St. Helens' eruption softened the highway's impact for awhile. But with restrictions lifted, hordes from the coast can be expected to flood into this high country on trips that now take only a matter of hours.

The lakes, meadows and huckleberry fields in these high elevation hills weren't built by nature to stand much stress from human use. Recreation facilities here were overtaxed even before the highway was built. What will happen now is anybody's guess.

There are only a handful of attractions to slow the visitor on a high-country trip. But they should all be savoured and enjoyed.

LOWER LEWIS RIVER FALLS

To some, the most beautiful spot in this part of the Gifford Pinchot.

Either hike a mile along a pleasant river trail from the highway, or a few hundred yards downstream from an undeveloped campground loop.

Find the trail from Highway 90 just below the bridge across the Lewis River near Cussed Hollow Creek. Trail starts to the right on the north side of the bridge and then follows the river upstream to the falls in a mile.

From the campground loop make your way to the river trail and then follow it downstream to the falls in only 100 yards. Listen to it before you start. Risky for children.

UPPER LEWIS RIVER FALLS

Still another torrent just off the highway.

See this falls at the end of a short and steep trail south of Highway 90 about a half-mile south of logging road junction to road No. 93.

STRAIGHT CREEK FALLS

A pretty waterfall just 2 miles by trail from Highway 90.

Drive about 17 miles from the Swift Reservoir to the bridge over Quartz Creek. Find the trail north of the road on the left side of the stream.

Hike through pleasant forest past Platinum Creek and then Straight Creek. See the falls upstream to the left. A falls on Quartz Creek, too, on the right of the trail below Straight Creek.

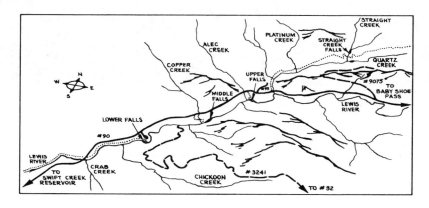

Huckleberry pickers

TWIN FALLS

This clutch of waterfall is within yards of the freeway-like forest highway.

Drive southerly on Highway 90 from the 90/23 junction, just south of Baby Shoe Pass, and watch for a gravel pit turnoff on the south side of the road.

You'll find the falls off a small campground just behind the piles of gravel. Sometimes you can drive through the pit area into the camp. (See page 184.)

LEWIS RIVER TRAIL

Just a sample here. But worth every bit of it.

Instead of hiking upstream along the Lewis River to see the Lower Lewis River Falls (see above), go downstream, crossing Cussed Hollow Creek and then wandering along the river as far as your heart directs you. Eventually the trail ends near Curly Creek. (See page 210.)

Flower fields near Bench Lake and Mt. Adams

S   MT. ADAMS,
SOUTH

TIMBERLINE

High meadows spread out near timberline on Mt. Adams' south slopes. Much of the area's beauty, however, falls victim to cattle each summer.

Drive to Trout Lake either from Randle via the Trout Lake-Randle road (No. 23) or from Vancouver via Highway 14 along the north shore of the Columbia. From Trout Lake drive north, turning right in about 1 mile and then left onto road No. 80 in another half-mile and then left on road No. 8051 in 2.5 miles. Road ends, very roughly, at Cold Springs Camp.

Cattle are permitted to graze the southwest slopes of the mountain each summer. Sheep graze allotments on west and north slopes. All of which bring modest grazing fees into the public treasury.

To appreciate the effect of grazing, compare vegetation near Timberline with the lush flower fields in the fenced Bird Creek Meadows 3.5 miles to the east.

CAMPGROUNDS

Morrison Creek — 11 units in a grassy, open timber area fenced against cattle. No views. Popular climbers' camp, often crowded with large parties. Pit toilets. 10.3 miles north of Trout Lake.

Cold Springs — A single shelter and several tables in a small corral-like area. Spring downhill from parking

loop about 200 feet. Turn off on short spur road about 12.9 miles from Trout Lake.

BIRD CREEK

The best is here. And treat it kindly, please. Now all part of the Yakima Indian Reservation. A use fee may be charged.

And don't ask for anything more. Not better roads. Or better trails. What man has built already is enough. Any further improvements endanger the fragile beauty. Man here can't add a single thing. So be satisfied with what God's wrought.

From Trout Lake drive north, following a blacktop road to the end. Turn right onto road No. 82 and then left onto road No. 80. Bird Creek Meadows in about 17.3 miles from Trout Lake.

CAMPGROUNDS

Bench Lake — 34 units at 4850 feet in timber around Bench Lake, some with a partial view of Mt. Adams. Entrance road not recommended for trailers. Swimming. Boat ramp. Piped water. Pit toilets. Fee.

Bird Lake — 20 units at 5500 feet situated in sparse timber. Views of Adams from some sites on the south side. Swimming. Pit toilets. Fee.

Mirror Lake — 7 sites on a small man-made lake at 5300 feet. Partial view of Mt. Adams. Busy and tends to be dusty as everyone seems to drive through on way toward the mountain. Piped water. Pit toilets. Fee.

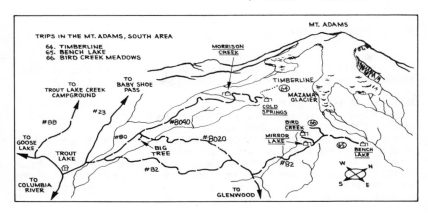

Sheep at Mud Flats

64   TIMBERLINE

High meadows, just below timberline.

Drive north from Trout Lake, turning left off pavement in about 1.5 miles onto roads No. 80 and 8051. Drive to the end and then hike 1.5 miles to Timberline. 🚐

ROUND-THE-MOUNTAIN TRAIL

Ever-changing views of Adams with glimpses of the Trout Creek valley, Mt. Hood, St. Helens, Three Sisters, and Jefferson.

Find trail to the left from the end of the road-trail at Timberline. Watch for sign. Hike as far as you please. Lug a pack and camp if you'd like.

Trail with minor ups and downs follows a fairly constant grade toward the west side of the mountain. Cattle often destroy meadow growth at the start of the trail, but are supposed to be kept out of the trail area after less than 1 mile. The cows, however, do not always read allotment agreements. 🚶

SALT CREEK

Calcium-incrusted plants and rocks along cold, mineral-water mountain streams.

Hike 2.8 miles west from Timberline along the Round-the-Mountain Trail (see above) to any of several branches of Salt Creek.

Watch for creeks after trail reaches Crofton Ridge area with views toward Sleeping Beauty. The creek displays are small and fragile. Sheepmen dubbed the stream Salt Creek due to the laxative effect of the mineral water.

CLIMBER'S TRAIL

A well-used climber's trail climbs to better and better views out of Timberline.

Follow old road trace toward the mountain as far as the trail is well-defined. About 1.5 miles. Don't attempt to go farther on the mountain unless you are equipped and knowledgeable. Pack trains once hauled gear to mining claims (sulfur) at the summit. ⚡

BIG TREE

The largest ponderosa pine in this area—198 feet high and 84 inches in diameter.

Turn right (east) off road No. 80 onto road No. 8020 about 2.5 miles north of the paved road junction. Marked tree on the right in about .25 miles.

If you also need to know the value of the preserved tree, it contains 22,000 board feet of lumber. 🚗

Nearest camping

Timberline, Morrison Creek, Cold Springs

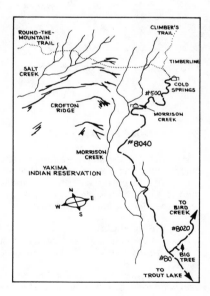

Bird Creek Meadows and Mt. Adams

65   BENCH LAKE

Hike to high mountain-meadow lakes, viewpoints, and down timbered trails — all
below a towering Adams in the Yakima Indian Reservation.

From Trout Lake drive north, following the blacktop road to the end. Turn right onto
road No. 82 and then left to Bird Creek. Bench Lake at the end of the road, not
recommended for trailers. 18.2 miles from Trout Lake.

BIRD CREEK FALLS

A cooling tumble of small cascades just off the road.

Drive **south** from Mirror Lake Campground (15.4 miles from Trout Lake) about 1.75
miles.

Park in a wide area north of the bridge and climb over rock slabs either above or
below the road, selecting your own best section of falls from the many small torrents
offered.

SHADOW LAKE TRAIL

Take your compass and follow a dimly-blazed trail to a small lake and a big
reflection of Mt. Adams. Less than 1.5 miles.

Hike down an old barred road east, opposite the turnoff to Bird Lake Campground.
Follow the now-abandoned road toward a slate mine (if you get to the mine you've

gone too far); watching for a faint sheep wagon trail to the right shortly before the road crosses the only full-time stream on the road. Look for blazes before you start.

A difficult trail to follow unless you keep constant watch for old blazes. If you can't see a blaze ahead of you, turn back and start again. Eventually the trail leads to old shepherd's camp signed "Lake Camp." Shadow Lake about 300 yards north of the sign.

(The lake can also be reached off the Cress Cabin trail-road from the junction of Bird Creek Meadows road. Watch for a small wet meadow south of the old road. Follow the drainage downhill about a half-mile to the lake.)

LITTLE MT. ADAMS
Breathtaking views of the bigger mountain from the top of the smaller one.

Take trail out of Bench Lake Campground (watch for sign away from the lake off the campground road on the north side). Trail drops down over Hellroaring Creek, then climbs about a half-mile to a ridge top.

Continue on trail to old sheep camp at Island Springs (2.5 miles from the lake) or climb open slopes to the west to reach the top of Little Mt. Adams at 6815 feet — a red cindercone crater that looks like a Roman stadium from a distance. Also about 2.5 miles.

BENCH LAKE TRAIL
Hike a mile around the lake with occasional glimpses of Mt. Adams and Little Mt. Adams over the lake.

Find trail through the campground on either side of the lake.

Swimming area in shallows at the east end of the lake.

HELLROARING MEADOWS
Hike across subalpine meadows to Heart Lake (1.5 miles) for awesome views up at Adams below Mazama Glacier.

Find trail off the left side of the Hellroaring Viewpoint about .25 mile west of Bench Lake. Viewpoint on loop spur off the north side of the road.

No need to end your trip at the lake. Explore increasingly open meadows toward the mountain for continuing interesting views. No trails. To the north find Little Mt. Adams and the Ridge of Wonders.

Nearest camping
Bench Lake, Bird Lake, Mirror Lake

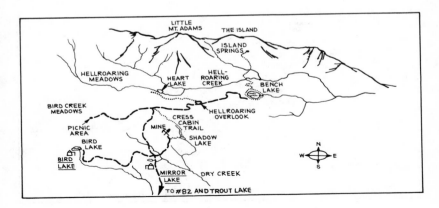

66 BIRD CREEK MEADOWS

If beauty is a comparative thing, then Bird Creek Meadows must be perfection.
From Trout Lake, drive north 15.4 miles to the Mirror Lake Campground, following the blacktop road to the end. Turn right onto road No. 82 and then left on Bird Creek road. Park below the Bird Creek Meadows Picnic Area about 1.1 miles beyond Mirror Lake and Mirror Lake Campground.

Meadows in every direction. All above 6000 feet. A use fee may be charged.

The largest assortment of alpine wildflowers in the world — over 400 varieties — pour out over open meadows in a vivid stream of color. Rock flowers — depending on the snow — appear in mid-July. The meadow flower season extends from mid-July to mid-September — again depending on the weather — with blooming at its best about mid-August.

And don't leave once you've seen the mountain. No single view tells the story here. Mt. Adams towering above flower color only opens the spectacle. So wander awhile. Savor the best in the hundreds of intimate glimpses — without the peak — of flowers posed against rock slopes, bracketed by alpine firs, hidden in rocky clefts, exploding along boggy stream beds, and framing glistening waterfalls.

A symphony!

NATURE LOOP

An easy 2-mile loop trail through a prime sampling of the splendor offered here.

Find trail at the entrance of the picnic area, near the main parking lot. Follow the Round-the-Mountain Trail about 200 yards west to a junction with Trail of the Flowers. Turn right and follow trail above picnic area, returning to the parking lot.

Views of Hood and Jefferson in Oregon when Adams is hidden to the north. And stay on the trails! Heavy foot traffic on fragile meadows like these soon destroys all plant life.

HELLROARING OVERLOOK

Pick your way over dry alpine slopes to a cliff's edge overlooking Hellroaring Meadows, the Mazama Glacier, and a mountainside of waterfalls.

Take spur trail off Nature Loop (see above). Watch for a tourist trail toward the mountain about 50 yards west of a point where loop trail ducks around a small cliff, about midway around the loop.

Wind-shaped alpine trees and small clinging flowers cover rockslab slopes leading to the cliff's edge. Explore the high ridge as you like.

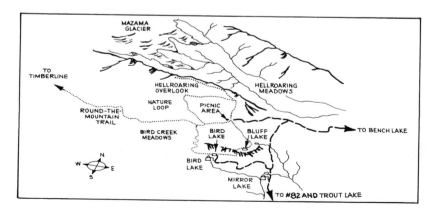

Hellroaring Overlook

BIRD LAKE TRAIL

Hike past several small waterfalls through a whole series of flower meadows.

Trail links Bird Lake and Bird Creek Meadows. From Bird Lake turn off at Mirror Lake onto road to Bird Lake Campground — find trail across small dam complex in southwest corner of the lake, hiking 1.5 miles gradually uphill, turning right toward Bird Creek, another .75 mile.

From Bird Creek Meadows take the Round-the-Mountain Trail west (follow blazes to avoid confusion of heavy tourist trails) for about .75 mile, turning downhill on Bird Lake Trail.

Allow plenty of time, either way. Not because the trail's difficult. But because each meadow, each creek, each waterfall offers its own miniature glimpse of beauty. A walk to be taken even if you've never walked before.

BLUFF LAKE TRAIL

Frame the reflection of Mt. Adams in shafts of bear grass, then turn, walking only a few feet, to a cliff-view south over Mirror Lake and the Bird Creek valley.

Find trail off turnaround in the northeast corner of the Bird Lake Campground picnic area. Trail drops away from the lake, crossing a small creek before climbing toward Bluff Lake.

Trail passes a spring that pours directly out of rock before reaching the lake. Continue around the lake to inlet-outlet streams (both are within several feet of each other), finding a tourist trail on the east side of the lake which leads to the far (south) end of the lake.

Views of Adams from the south end. Climb the ridge behind the lake to look down on the valley. Higher points to the right yield views of Mt. Hood, too.

Nearest camping

Mirror Lake, Bird Lake, Bench Lake

T CENTRAL PINCHOT

If you ever wondered why the Indians so loved the Mt. Adams country, the reason is here. High huckleberry meadows, vistas, and lakes — all watched over by the most spectacular mountain package in the West — Rainier, Adams, and St. Helens, all at once.

Drive to Trout Lake either via forest road from Randle and Packwood or by Highway 14 up the Columbia River from Vancouver.

From Trout Lake drive west past the Mt. Adams Ranger Station on road No. 24, either turning north in about a mile onto road No. 88 or continuing on road No. 24 as it swings north at the Peterson Guard Station. Twin Buttes are in about 24 miles.

(All sorts of new paved roads spring up in this area constantly. But if you follow the old roads you can get there too. With less rush.)

CAMPGROUNDS

Little Goose — 28 sites in timber. Popular with berrypickers, hikers, and riders into Indian Heaven backcountry. Piped water. Pit toilets. 15.3 miles from Trout Lake.

Cultus Creek — 65 units on several loops under an open canopy of trees. Piped water. Pit toilets. 17.5 miles from Trout Lake. Fee.

Meadow Creek, Cold Springs, Surprise Lakes — Primitive Indian campgrounds in Indian-only huckleberry picking area east of road. Use only in off-season.

South — 8 units. A relatively primitive camp. Pit toilets. 23.5 miles from Trout Lake.

Saddle — 12 sites on loop road No. 2480 off No. 24 at Twin Buttes. Pit toilets. 24.5 miles from Trout Lake.

Tillicum — 49 sites. Piped water. Pit toilets. 24 miles from Trout Lake. Fee.

Twin Falls — 7 units in heavy timber near a noisy waterfall. Secluded but often busy. Pit toilets. About 35 miles from Trout Lake via roads No. 88 and No. 200.

Peterson Prairie — 19 sites along a slow stream in a pleasant timbered area. A sheltered camp away from roads. Piped water. Pit toilets. 7.4 miles west of Trout Lake on No. 24. Fee.

Smoky Creek — 3 units in a wooded area on Smoky Creek. Piped water. Pit toilets. 13.7 miles from Trout Lake on No. 24.

Sleeping Beauty and Mt. Adams

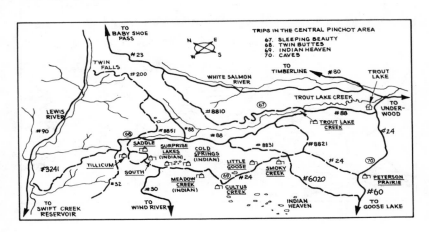

TRIPS IN THE CENTRAL PINCHOT AREA

67. SLEEPING BEAUTY
68. TWIN BUTTES
69. INDIAN HEAVEN
70. CAVES

TO BABY SHOE PASS

TWIN FALLS

#23

#200

N E W S

WHITE SALMON RIVER

TO TIMBERLINE #80 TROUT LAKE

LEWIS RIVER

#90

#8810

67

TROUT LAKE CREEK

TO UNDER-WOOD

#88

TROUT LAKE CREEK

#24

#8851

#88

66

#88

SADDLE

SURPRISE LAKES (INDIAN)

COLD SPRINGS (INDIAN)

#8831

#8821

#24

70

#3241

TILLICUM

SOUTH

LITTLE GOOSE

SMOKY CREEK

PETERSON PRAIRIE

#32

MEADOW CREEK (INDIAN)

69

#24

CULTUS CREEK

#6020

#60

TO SWIFT CREEK RESERVOIR

#30

TO WIND RIVER

INDIAN HEAVEN

TO GOOSE LAKE

67 SLEEPING BEAUTY

Hike to one view, drive to several, and search out a waterfall northwest of Trout Lake.

From Trout Lake, drive west on state highway 141 past the Mt. Adams Ranger Station, turning right (north) onto road No. 88 about a mile beyond the station. Road No. 8810 junction in another 3.9 miles.

From Randle, take the Trout Lake-Randle road (No. 23) over Baby Shoe Pass, turning right onto road No. 8810 about 10.2 miles south of the pass.

SLEEPING BEAUTY VISTA

Certainly not a straight but a very narrow and scenic path to heaven. Old lookout site on a basalt column, 5076 feet high.

From junction with road No. 88, drive north on road No. 8810, turning right in about 6.4 miles onto the Beauty Pit road. Watch for trail sign on uphill side in a clearcut. About a half-mile.

Trail starts in the clearcut, climbing into timber area with no views until it suddenly breaks out at the base of a basalt shaft. Path to the top of the shaft has been blasted out of rock in a steep switchback-like series of ramps. No building. No restraints. No place for small children.

Views of Adams, Rainier, St. Helens, Hood, and the Trout Lake valley from the very top. The basalt spire is the "nose" of a sleeping beauty that Trout Lake natives say lies across their valley below Adams. Look northwest for it as you enter Trout Lake from the south. Her head is to the northeast. Her body spreads out below Mt. Adams to the southwest. ✝

NINEFOOT VIEWS

A closeup view of Mt. Adams on a logging road just off the main Trout Lake-Randle road (No. 23).

From Randle, continue over Baby Shoe Pass on road No. 23, turning right onto Ninefoot road No. 2360 4.3 miles beyond the junction with road No. 8810.

From Trout Lake, drive north toward the mountain, following signs bearing left to road No. 23. Turn left onto Ninefoot road in 9 miles.

Drive about a half-mile up the road for views up at the southwest slope of Adams, the Avalanche and Pinnacle Glaciers.

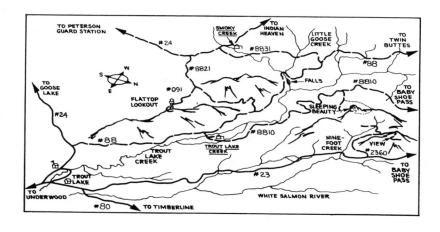

Sleeping Beauty Mountain from road No. 8810

FLATTOP

Drive to a state lookout site for split views of all the major peaks in this region.

From the 88/8810 junction (see above), drive northwesterly on road No. 88 turning left onto road No. 8821 in about 1.7 miles. Vista spur in another 3.1 miles. Watch for signs.

To reach the point from Peterson Campground, drive north on road No. 24 about 4.6 miles, turning right onto road No. 8821, lookout spur No. 091. Views of Adams, Rainier and Hood.

To add St. Helens, drive across the flattop mountain to an open-meadow view that includes — again — Rainier and Adams.

LITTLE GOOSE CREEK FALLS

For adults only. But a show that no waterfall collector will want to miss — even though you can't get close.

Follow road No. 88 (see above) beyond the road No. 2420 (old N67) junction past Little Goose Creek. After crossing the bridge, follow road, parking where it turns sharply away from the creek.

No trail. Walk out the ridge, parallel to the creek about 75 yards, then make your way cautiously toward the rim of the cliff-sided canyon, listening and looking back upstream for the falls. Bare gravel marks along the rim are NOT viewpoints but places where the ground has sifted over the cliff!

The falls — deep in the canyon and never officially measured — plunge some 100-plus feet in a startling but very private display of forest beauty.

Not for small children or skittish adults. 🚶

Nearest camping

Peterson, Smoky Creek, Little Goose

68   TWIN BUTTES

Drive west out of Trout Lake past the Mt. Adams Ranger Station on road No. 24, continuing on road No. 24 along the edge of Indian Heaven country to Twin Buttes and Twin Falls.

Or take a shortcut, turning north off road No. 24 about a mile west of the Ranger Station onto road No. 88 following it to a junction with road No. 200 in the midst of the area.

Twin Falls about 24 miles by the 88/200 roads.

LANGFIELD FALLS

A short walk to an instant reminder of what beautiful forests are all about. Just off road No. 88 about 14 miles from Trout Lake where it jogs sharply north at its intersection with road No. 8851: (No. 8851 continues straight ahead.)

From a parking lot about .1 mile north of the turn (on the right) follow a gentle trail into pleasant forest as it winds down to the bottom of a very pretty, very cool and very noisy waterfall.

The trail was developed in memory of K. C. Langfield, ranger in the Mt. Adams district between 1933 and 1956.

WEST TWIN BUTTE

All that's best in this area's high views from a lookout site you can almost drive to.

Take road No. 2480 loop road to Saddle Campground off road No. 24 either north or south of the butte. Spur to the butte viewpoint uphill (west) just south of the Saddle Campground.

Road ends just below the former lookout site. Short spurts of switchbacks lead to a vista point looking out on St. Helens, Adams and Rainier.

TWIN FALLS

Pretty, talkative torrents near a remote camping area on the upper reaches of the Lewis River.

Unmaintained camping spots south of the river at the end of road No. 200. Find this road to the right off road No. 88 roughly 4 miles north of Langfield Falls.

Falls upstream. The campground across the river can be reached from forest Highway 90, but it's unsigned behind a gravel pit. (See page 171.)

STEAMBOAT ROCK

From a cliffside viewpoint at 5425 feet look out on a circle of volcanic peaks — Adams, St. Helens, Rainier, with the Goat Rocks in the background.

Drive northwest past Mosquito Lakes on road No. 8851, turning sharply east onto road No. 8854 and turning off left again onto road No. 021, leading to a gravel pit.

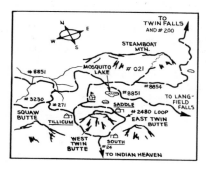

Steamboat Mountain and Mt. Adams from West Twin Butte

A new trailhead is planned to the left of the road. If you can't find it, drive to the gravel pit and climb uphill, to the left, at the pit entrance finding the trail above the road.

Use care in parking if the gravel pit is in use and care in hiking through this formal Natural Area. Vistas in .75 mile.

Nearest camping
Tillicum, Saddle, South, Lewis River Shelter, Cultus Creek, Twin Falls

Indian Camp at one of the Surprise Lakes

69   INDIAN HEAVEN

All trail country this. A high plateau sparkling with lakes and brilliant huckleberry meadows. **But** pressed already by paved roads and supermarket-size paved parking lots.

From Trout Lake, drive west past the Mt. Adams Ranger Station, following road No. 88 north to Mosquito Lakes and then south around West Twin Butte to the northern part of the meadows.

From Wind River, drive northwest past the Carson National Fish Hatchery, turning north onto road No. 30 and the west side of Indian Heaven country.

HUCKLEBERRY MEADOWS

One of the few places where the Indian still has something to himself — even though it's much less than he is entitled to.

Indians have exclusive huckleberry rights on the east side of road No. 24. The White Man, with his usual graciousness, took everything else.

Stay out during huckleberry season. But at other times explore meadows around Surprise Lakes — 15 shallow ponds — for continually-changing views of the countryside. Pacific Crest Trail cuts through meadows.

INDIAN VIEWPOINT

A signed road view of towering Mt. Adams and its foothill system including Sleeping Beauty.

Drive north from road No. 24 about .6 mile north of Cultus Creek Guard Station. Sign on the right.

For a more surprising view drive another 3.1 miles to the crest of the Cascade Range at 4250 feet. Rainier and St. Helens suddenly join the scene with Adams.

SAWTOOTH MOUNTAIN
A 2-mile trail starts out in huckleberry fields and then winds its way up the side of Sawtooth Mountain for views out in every direction.

Start south on the Pacific Crest Trail where it crosses road No. 24 about a half-mile south of its junction with paved road No. 30.

After an easy mile follow a spur trail uphill on a series of switchbacks that lead first to views out to the east over the Surprise Lakes and the Indian huckleberry fields toward Mt. Adams and finally to high vistas toward the west of Indian Heaven and St. Helens.

Turn back at the high point of the trail along the west face of the mountain. In the fall, leave plenty of time for eating berries.

PLACID LAKE
An easy walk of a little more than a half-mile leads to Placid Lake, which is exactly what the name implies. Walk another mile to a more private view of Chenamus Lake.

Find the trail to the south off road No. 420 after turning east from road No. 30 about 6 miles south of its junction with road No. 24 on the northern end of Indian Heaven.

The trail drops gradually through forest to a meadow cove on Placid Lake. Camp or picnic spots nearby.

To reach Chenamus Lake, follow a trail left (east) along Placid Lake taking a spur right (south) in only a few yards. The path here wanders through small meadows before reaching Chenamus Lake. Camp spots here too.

CLUSTER LAKES
Too many lakes here to name. Some not even on the trail. But a hike of less than 2 miles will lead you right into the middle of them.

(Don't be frightened by all the cars parked along the road. This area soaks up people like a sponge.)

To find the trail, turn south off road No. 30 onto road No. 65 (N605) about a half-mile

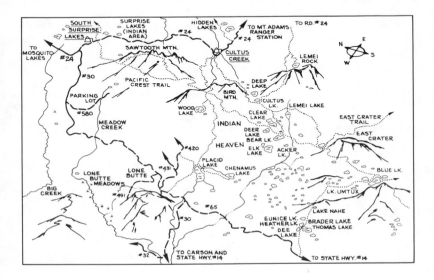

south of the Placid Lake turnoff (see above). Trailhead in another 3 miles.

The trail, on the east side of the road, climbs through a clearcut and then uphill to Dee Lake (north of the trail) and Thomas Lake (to the south of it), all within about .75 mile.

From here on the choices are all yours. Go straight ahead down a short spur to Eunice Lake. Or follow the main trail uphill in spurts past some lakes and near others reaching Lake Nahe in about 2 miles.

Believe the occasional signs that point to lakes you can't see. Brader Lake, for instance, lies just over a ridge. No trail, but it's worth the trip. Maps identify still other lakes with neither signs nor trails.

The path goes on to Blue Lake in a total of 3.5 miles. Still more lakes along the way.

Nearest camping

Cultus Creek, Meadow Creek, South, Tillicum, Saddle, Little Goose, Smoky Creek

Note: The big parking areas, south of road No. 30 on paved road spur No. 580 (berry field access) west of the junction with road No. 24, aren't for camping, although you'll often find campers there. Theoretically (and very expensively) these parking lots and picnic areas were built for day-use-only berry pickers, who visit here only in the fall.

Hopefully, the whole mess has been overdesigned. If as many people come as are provided for, the meadow system will certainly soon be overrun.

70   CAVES

Only two are listed here but cave explorers have found many more in this same area of Skamania County.

Drive west from Trout Lake on Highway 141 past the Mt. Adams Ranger Station to road No. 24 and the Peterson Campground.

Big Cave, Curley Creek Cave, Dry Creek Cave, Lemei Road Cave, and New Cave are some of the named ones. For details on most of the caves and their locations, see **Caves of Washington,** by William R. Halliday, published by the Washington Department of Conservation, Division of Mines and Geology, Olympia, Wash. At the library.

Unless you are properly equipped and trained in exploring caves, don't. Cave prowling, like mountain climbing, requires skills best learned in organized schools. ⫚

ICE CAVE

Carry a flashlight or lantern and climb down a ladder into a natural freezer, glistening with ice even in late summer.

Turn south off road No. 24 about 5.8 miles west of Trout Lake, following cave signs to parking area near the hole-in-the-ground entrance.

Find ice formations to the left (east) of the ladder in a dead-end Crystal Grotto and ice pool. Ice stalactites sometimes hang from the cave ceiling. But most often they're

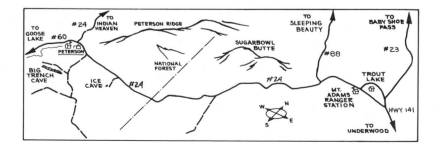

destroyed by vandals early in the season. Shaft to the right of the ladder leads some 600 feet underground. Don't explore unless you're equipped.

BIG TRENCH CAVE

Explore the collapsed remnants of a lava tube cave system that once stretched 4000 feet underground.

The lave tube caves, common in this area, were formed when the tops of lava flows cooled and solidified, allowing the still-molten inner mass to continue flowing, leaving a hollow tube.

Turn right (east) out of Peterson Campground, taking the first logging road to the right (south) in about a half-mile. Watch for an old logging spur to the right in the middle of the first clearcut. The trench parallels the road about 100 yards further south.

Hike into the clearcut watching for signs of lava outcrops. Ceiling sections of the cave have collapsed in spots, forming deep gullies. Underground shafts still link the fallen sections. Find entranceways through debris or simply (and safely) appreciate the violence that formed such caves from surface level. Again, don't explore the caves unless you are equipped and trained in the ways of caves. ⭫

Nearest camping

Peterson, Lost Creek

Ice Cave near Peterson Guard Station

Goose Lake

U   GOOSE LAKE

A mixture of legendary footprints, old Indian race tracks, lakes, lookouts, and lava.

Easiest and quickest way to reach this area from Seattle is via Vancouver and state Highway 14 through either Trout Lake, Willard, or Carson.

From Trout Lake drive west on Highway 141 past the Mt. Adams Ranger Station to road No. 24, turning off onto 60 at the Peterson Campground. Goose Lake in 12.7 miles from Trout Lake.

From Carson, drive north on county road No. 8C, turning right onto forest road No. 65 in about 4.5 miles. Goose Lake in another 16.7 miles.

From Willard, drive north past the former Willard Ranger Station complex, turning left onto road No. 66 in about .25 mile. Goose Lake in 15 miles more.

CAMPGROUNDS

Goose Lake — 25 sites on a loop road above the lake. Pleasant camp in timber. Most camp units on a steep hillside. Lug gear from the road. Piped water. Pit toilets. Boat launching. Campground trails.

Black Creek — 3 units in remote area near, but not on, Black Creek. Usually occupied. Pit toilets. On road No. 60 about 23 miles from Carson or 2.5 miles west of spur to Red Mountain Lookout and Race Track.

71 FORLORN LAKES

Acres of lakes, lava, and a mysterious footprint in a lake bottom.

GOOSE LAKE FOOTPRINT

Legend has it that a pretty Indian maid jumped off the top of a nearby mountain while fleeing a troublesome lover, landing in molten lava, leaving her hand and moccasin-prints there for posterity. (After the berry season, the story goes, she can be seen sitting on a rock by the lake, combing her hair.)

As difficult to find as to believe. But at extreme low water look for the prints on a lava point off the northeast shore. Only visible at extreme low water in the fall and sometimes, then, they may be filled with silt. Aluminum tags on two Douglas firs give compass bearings to the prints.

There's no doubt the imprints are the right size. Many modernday maids have tried them on. But legend-shatterers tend to believe a lonesome trapper carved them, hoping, probably, some Indian maid might (not did) jump into them. Time turned his story around.

LAVA FLOWS

Trees have already started to overgrow a massive lava flow south of Goose Lake. But much of the original violence can still be appreciated.

From Goose Lake Campground turn left on road No. 60 and then right in about .25 mile onto road No. 6621, driving to South Prairie. Lava flows to the right of the road south of the prairie.

The road follows the hillside that blocked the flow. Watch for strange shapes that seem to have been frozen only moments ago. Stop and explore. But don't wander far. There are no trails. One ridge looks just like another here and getting lost is easy. Be careful, too, of unexpected cracks. ⚡

FORLORN LAKES

A dozen small lakes set in less than a mile-square area.

From Goose Lake Campground turn left on road No. 60 and then left again uphill on road No. 6040. If you wish, return via road No. 6035 to road No. 60.

The timbered lakes lie on both sides of the road. Two of the larger lakes lie on the left (northwest) of the road. Watch through the trees. Find your own way. Most of the smaller lakes lie to the right of the road within .25 mile. Unmarked fisherman trails. Best in late fall. Summer mosquitoes can be devastating.

Nearest camping

Goose Lake, Lost Creek, Black Creek

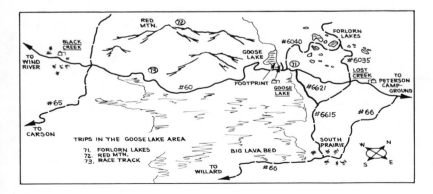

72   RED MOUNTAIN

Big peaks galore and a lava tube cave more than a mile long.
Start from Goose Lake Campground on road No. 60.

LAVA CAVES

A 6000-foot lava tube cave, called Lava Cave on forest maps, but called Falls Creek Cave and Panther Creek Cave in cave journals.

From Goose Lake Campground turn right onto road No. 60, driving to a junction with road No. 65 in about 6.5 miles. Turn right on road No. 65 and then left on road No. 67. In less than a mile turn right on road No. 6701 and find the trail beyond the rock pit off a short spur road.

No place here for amateurs. Explore only if you are equipped and know what you're doing. Ice floors, brick red lava, chimneys, and side spurs. For details see **Caves of Washington,** by William R. Halliday, Washington Department of Conservation, Division of Mines and Geology, Olympia, Wash.

RED MOUNTAIN LOOKOUT

From a huckleberry hill topped with red volcanic cinders see Rainier, Adams, St. Helens, Hood, and as far south as Mt. Jefferson in Oregon.

From Goose Lake Campground turn right on road No. 60, turning right again in about 5 miles onto road No. 6048. The road leads to the top of the mountain. Expect heavy silt.

A lookout with sweeping vistas out over the hills and ridges of the Indian Heaven country. A spectacular sight.

PACIFIC CREST TRAIL

Southern gateway to the Indian Heaven country and trips up the Pacific Crest Trail to Mt. Adams and into the Goat Rocks.

From Goose Lake Campground turn right onto road No. 60. Watch for horse-loading ramps and well-signed trails just before road reaches the Red Mountain Lookout road.

No short hikes here. But the trail, in about 2 miles, passes several small open meadows — without additional spectacle.

Nearest camping

Goose Lake, Black Creek, Lost Creek

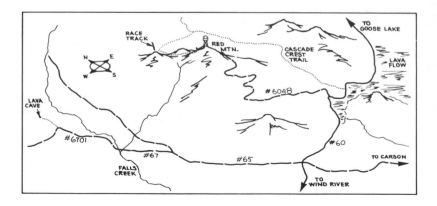

Mt. Hood from Red Mountain

U GOOSE LAKE

73 RACE TRACK

Compute for yourself the number of years it must have taken for horsemen to beat this path across a high mountain meadow.

From Goose Lake Campground turn right on road No. 60, driving to the Red Mountain Lookout road in about 15 miles. Find trail to the Race Track on curve just below the lookout parking area. On the right. A 1.5-mile hike, easy going in but stiff climbing coming out.

Find the .25-mile track pounded out across the meadow where the trail forks to the right. Shallow lakes in the meadow area early in the year.

For glimpses of the track without hiking into the meadow, drop down the trail about .25 mile to a saddle between Red Mountain and a knoll. Climb the knoll. Viewpoint just over the top. An early-morning or late-afternoon sun shows the track at its best.

Ernie Childs, former recreation technician with the Mt. Adams District of Gifford Pinchot National Forest, reports that the last races were held during the Prohibition era.

"Several horsemen of this vicinity and the lower Yakima valley trained horses especially for the event, betting moonshine whiskey against money, horses, or whatever the Indians had," Childs said.

The race ended against a steep hill so horses would stop.

Nearest camping
Goose Lake

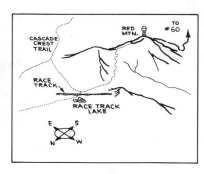

Deeply-worn Race Track made by Indians many years ago

Indian Race Track from a shoulder of Red Mountain

Road to Government Mineral Springs

V   WIND RIVER

Primarily a timber-harvest area but with the saving graces of view roads, meadows, lookouts, old cinder cones, soda springs, and lakes.

From Vancouver, drive east along the Columbia River on Highway 14, turning north at Carson on the county road. Wind River Ranger Station, 10 miles from Carson.

CAMPGROUNDS

Little Soda Springs — 4 sites in a soggy and shady hardwood area near the Wind River. A walk-in camp. Park on a loop near a pump and carry your gear across a footbridge to campsite. Pump water. Soda spring. Pit toilet. 18 miles from Carson on road No. 5401.

Panther Creek — 22 sites in young forest area near Panther Creek. Pit toilets. Stream water. 10 miles from Carson on road No. 65. Fee.

Paradise — 31 sites on pleasant parklike loops near the Wind River. Trails to the river. A new camp. Pump water. Pit toilets. 20 miles from Carson on road No. 30. Fee.

Beaver — 20 sites in a heavily-shaded, somewhat-brushy river bottom. Some sites on the Wind River. Group camps on reservation. Others on loops away from the river. Piped water. Toilets. 12 miles from Carson on county road.

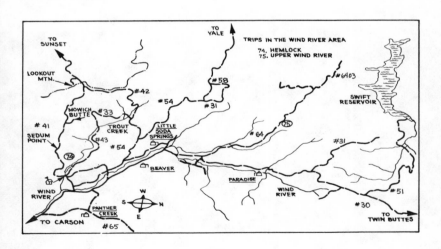

74   HEMLOCK LAKE

No camping here, but a great place to spend a summer afternoon if you're camping nearby. Trails, views, drives, nurseries.

Drive north from Carson on the county road, turning left in about 8 miles toward the Wind River Ranger Station. Hemlock Lake and ranger station in about 1.5 mile.

TREE NURSERY

60 million tree seedlings and a cone-processing operation that makes it all possible.

Find seedlings growing in fields both behind the ranger station and across the bridge south of the station.

The nursery ships about 22 million trees for planting each year and processes about 13,000 bushels of cones producing about 8,400 pounds of new seed. About 86,000 pounds of seed are stored in freezers as a hedge against poor seed years.

HEMLOCK LAKE

Picnicking but no camping. Swim from a supervised beach. Canoe into the upper byways of the man-made lake. Or prowl tourist trails around a dam and fish ladder at the lower end of the lake. Likely to be crowded on weekends.

WIND RIVER ARBORETUM

Find a lesson here in the sensitivity of nature and the oft-times futility of man's effort to improve on it. A half-mile hike.

Cross the bridge in front of the ranger station, turning uphill away from nursery fields, between the fourth and fifth houses. Trailhead and parking area near a log-section shelter.

The largest collection of conifers in the world, with trees transplanted from other areas, once thrived — some of them almost 40 years — and then died because

environmental extremes were just a little different than their natural seeding grounds. Markers along trails show where species died and why.

Get free booklet from ranger station before beginning your hiking tour. 🚶

NATURAL AREA TRAIL

No spectacle here. Simply the secrecy and privacy of an undisturbed virgin forest. A 2-mile trail.

Drive past the Wind River Ranger Station on road No. 43. Find trail to the right (watch for sign) in about 3 miles.

Trail leads through dense forest to road No. 5400, reaching the latter about 2 miles from the ranger station. A level trail.

MOWICH BUTTE

Rainier, St. Helens, Adams, Hood, and Jefferson over huckleberries, penstemon, beargrass, and tiger lilies.

Cross the bridge south of the ranger station, turning sharply right by the nursery onto road No. 41. Drive past the Forest Service shops and up a narrow, winding and rough road to the top of the ridge.

Uphill spurs lead to high views (if they're open). For other vistas, drive about 12 miles into a forest-fire area that has never recovered. Vistas everywhere.

Best views, however, from a three-way junction in about 18 miles. From the three-way junction either return or continue (take the left road) on road No. 41 to Sunset Campground. Again, it's a narrow, rough road which can be traveled by a modern passenger car — with care. Worth one trip, at least.

Nearest camping

Beaver, Little Soda Springs

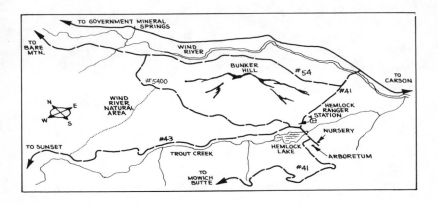

Wind River tree nursery

St. Helens from Point 3670

75 UPPER WIND RIVER

Views, meadows, and soda springs — all off road No. 30.
From Carson drive north on the county road, turning right onto road No. 30 about 14 miles from Carson and about 1 mile below Government Mineral Springs picnic area.

MINERAL SPRINGS

Two soda springs — one with a pump and another bubbling out of the ground.
Find both springs in upper end of Government Mineral Springs picnic area, at the end of county road. Follow signs.
Find the "Iron Mike" spring in a shelter to the left of a parking area. Pump as much of the spring water as you want.
To find "Bubbling Mike" and "Little Iron Mike" springs, take a 25-yard trail on the opposite side of the parking loop. Watch for sign on the right as you drive into the area. Trail leads to springs bubbling out of the ground.
Water contains calcium carbonate, sodium chloride, and calcium sulphate.

POINT 3670

One of the few high places that offers such a close-up look at the power of St. Helens' eruption.

Drive up the Wind River road No. 30 turning left on road No. 31 and onto road No. 3103. Viewpoint at the end of the road.

Look across at what's left of St. Helens, only 15 miles away, and the devastating mudflow down the Muddy River caused when the Shoestring Glacier suddenly turned to water.

The cascading mud flooded Smith Creek, wiping out two bridges, and flowed on into the upper end of the Swift Reservoir. North of the mountain, along the ridge overlooking Spirit Lake, note the miles and miles of total destruction.

In addition to St. Helens, views of Rainier, Adams and the Goat Rocks.

FALLS CREEK

Hike 2 miles along a creek to a triple falls on Falls Creek.

To find these trails, drive north from Wind River turning right onto road No. 30 and then right again onto road No. 3062 in less than a mile. At a fork near the end of the road, bear right onto road No. 057 to the end of the road.

Take the lower trail 152-A — the upper trail goes **above** the falls — following the path along the right side of the stream to the base of the falls.

Glimpses of all three falls before you get to the base of the lowest.

DRY CREEK FALLS

Walk only a half-mile here to the base of a cascade on Dry Creek.

From the county road junction, go north on road No. 30 about 2 miles to Dry Creek road No. 64. Turn left following road No. 64 to the bridge over Dry Creek. (It's signed.) Find the unmarked path off a parking area on the far side of the bridge — to the right. ⚲

Nearest camping

Paradise, Beaver, Some primitive camp spots near high meadows

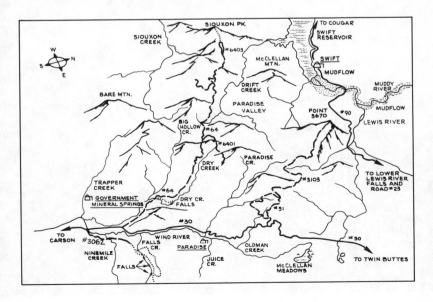

W   SUNSET

Waterfalls and a spectacular view south to Portland over the Columbia River Gorge. But limited by fire restrictions.

Drive south from Seattle-Tacoma-Olympia on I-5, turning east on Highway 503 at Woodland, 20 miles south of Kelso. Follow 503 east to Yale, then south across the Lewis River, past Chelatchie, to Amboy.

Silver Star Mountain

W SUNSET

At Amboy follow signs to Yacolt, turning left onto forest road No. 42 about 2.5 miles south of Yacolt. Sunset picnic area 10 miles from Yacolt.

This highway winds through some of the most scenic farm country in the state, with St. Helens looking over almost every valley. A pleasant drive even if you don't go on to the Sunset area.

SUNSET FALLS

The East Fork Lewis River tumbles 20 feet out of rock-scoured tubs and bowls into a clear blue pool where many people swim.

Drive to the Sunset picnic area on the right. Park there or drive another 100 yards or so to falls sign.

Follow tourist trails either to the pool below the falls or to the deeply-eroded rock slabs above. Deep bowls in the upper level make the most interesting prowling. ⊆⊃

SILVER STAR MOUNTAIN

If you're a lover of high places with truly unusual vistas — and willing to suffer for them — then put Silver Star near the top of your list.

Not only views of Rainier, Adams, St. Helens, Hood, Jefferson and even the Olympics, but also of Portland spread out as a living map at your feet.

And you can even drive to it, if you can stand all the bumps. A very, very rough road. At 5 miles an hour, in some places, you're speeding.

About 5 miles southeast of Yacolt (or 5 miles west of the Sunset Picnic Area) turn south off road No. 42 across the East Fork of the Lewis River onto the Dole road, turning right in about 2 miles onto a logging road. At a junction in about 7 miles turn uphill on road No. 4109. Lookout site in about 6 miles more.

Or from Sunset turn right off road No. 42 just east of the picnic-camping area onto road No. 41 following it to the lookout road spur No. 4109. Lookout in about 9.7 miles from Sunset.

Road No. 4109 to the lookout can be extremely rough. It ends just below a path to the former tower site (if you want to drive that far). Allow a day and lots of time for wondering why you started.

PITS

Nobody knows who dug them, much less why.

From Silver Star Lookout (see above) follow a spur trail south along the ridge line about a half-mile.

Find a half-dozen pits in loose talus betwen 5 and 6 feet deep. There's no obvious reason for the pits. Make up your own.

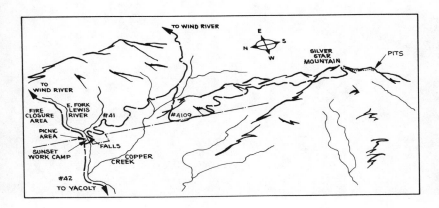

St. Helens from viewpoint near Yale Reservoir

X SOUTH ST. HELENS

A vast area of lava caves, tree casts, waterfalls, river trails, mountain meadows, and lakes in heavy timber country near the reservoir system on the Lewis River.

Drive south from Seattle-Tacoma-Olympia on I-5, turning east on Highway 503 at Woodland, 20 miles south of Kelso. At Yale, 23 miles from the freeway, continue east on Highway 90 to Cougar in 6 more miles, and the St. Helens Ranger Station, 18 miles from Cougar, 48 miles from I-5.

Note: Travel in much of this area could be restricted if St. Helens should start acting up again. So check with forest officials before planning any extended trips.

Expect heavy mid-week logging traffic. Some roads could be closed. Most roads, however, are open on weekends.

CAMPGROUNDS

Cougar — 45 tent-only sites in a camp maintained by the Pacific Power & Light Company. Restrooms. Piped water. On Yale Reservoir about 14 miles east of Yale.

Swift — 101 sites on wooded loop near Swift Creek Reservoir. Restrooms. Piped water. Boat launching. A heavy-use area operated by the Pacific Power & Light Company. Turn off 90 toward lake about .1 mile below ranger station.

Primitive sites — Some undeveloped, primitive campspots can be found near creeks and around open meadows. No developments. Find your own. Be extremely careful with fire.

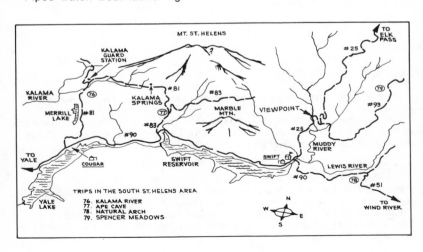

TRIPS IN THE SOUTH ST. HELENS AREA
76. KALAMA RIVER
77. APE CAVE
78. NATURAL ARCH
79. SPENCER MEADOWS

Yale Reservoir and St. Helens

76 KALAMA RIVER

Waterfalls, springs, marshes, and startling views of the damage south of St. Helens.

From I-5 drive east on Highway 503 to Yale, continuing on Highway 90 toward Cougar. Turn left (north) on road No. 81 about 5 miles from Yale (1 mile below Cougar), driving past Merrill Lake toward the Kalama Work Center.

KALAMA FALLS

A 40-foot sheet of water plunges over a lava cliff into a clear pool.

From 90 (the main road along the reservoirs) drive north 6.3 miles on road No. 81 (see above), turning left on Weyerhaeuser 7500 road.

Follow the timber company road west about 1 mile and then south (left) about .75 mile, watching for a crude sign or spur road on the right. (If you reach a curve to the right you've driven too far.)

Either park on the road or drive down short spur to a very small parking area near the falls. Find trail off the parking area. It heads downstream first, dropping over a bank and then turns upstream to the base of the falls.

Follow tourist trails for side views of the pretty torrent, watching for springs rolling out of the side of the cliff.

Falls, road, and parking area are all on private land. ⚊

KALAMA SPRINGS

A nearby campground was buried under three feet of mud during St. Helens' eruption. But the Kalama Springs kept right on running.

Find the springs to the right of the buried campground, now a picnic area. Continue north on road No. 81 (see above) and then eastward to McBride Lake. 12 miles from Highway 90.

The spring generates a full-blown river in less than 100 feet after flowing from beneath a lava cliff. Walk toward the cliff and the sounds of water. And don't forget to be awed by all that mud nearby.

GOAT MARSH

Open soggy meadows and lakes with views up at St. Helens. A 1-mile hike.

Drive north on road No. 81 past Merrill Lake and the Kalama Work Center to trailhead on left side of road. About 11 miles. Trail leads to shallow lakes southeast of Goat Mountain. Watch for elk.

Nearest camping

Cougar, Kalama Springs

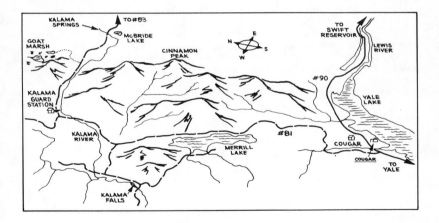

77 APE CAPE

Caves, tree casts on lava, and views of St. Helens from an area which the Forest Service seeks to classify as a geological recreation area.

Drive east from I-5 on Highway 503, continuing past Cougar on Highway 90, turning left (northerly) onto road No. 83 about 6 miles from Cougar (first road left beyond the Swift Creek Dam overlook).

LAVA TREE CASTS

Dozens of lava molds — some even show details of bark — created when molten lava flowed over a living forest hundreds of years ago.

Turn left off road No. 83 (see above) onto road No. 8303 about 1.7 miles from the 90 junction. Watch for Ape Cave signs.

Find tree past picnic area to the left (south) of road No. 8303 in timber just beyond the clearcut that begins at the junction, in less than .25 mile.

Tourist trails lead off a parking spur. Tree casts — deep tree-shaped holes or wells — within 100 to 150 yards. Several casts of fallen trees show clearest imprints of bark. Be careful where you step. Follow tourist trails. ⸙

APE CAVE

The longest lava-tube cave in the United States and one of the most popular and easy-to-find caves south of St. Helens.

Continue on road No. 8303 (see above) about 1 mile from the junction with road No. 83. Watch for a fenced area on the right. Parking area on left. Pit toilets.

Find large entrance inside fenced area, with stairs leading down into the cave.

The Ape Cave is more than 2 miles long (11,215 feet) and drops about 700 feet. No apes. Cave got its name from an exploring group that used that name. But there are bats.

Portions of the cave south of the entrance are considered safe; however, always take gas lantern, extra flashlight, hiking boots, hardhats, and warm clothing.

There are two levels in the cave with the top level passable in only a few places. Stay on the lower. Notice chockstone frozen in ceiling of lower cave about a half-mile from the entrance.

(The cave is one of about five in this same general area. For details on the others see **Caves in Washington**, William R. Halliday, Washington Department of Conservation, Olympia.) ⸙

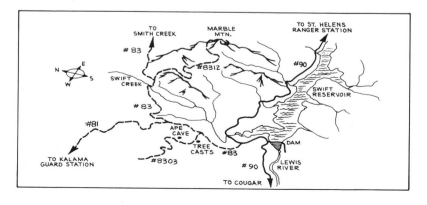

Main tube in Ape Cave

MARBLE MOUNTAIN VIEW

Reach out from 4128 feet and almost touch the sides of St. Helens. Look into the convulsed mud-choked valleys of Pine Creek and the Muddy River.

Turn right, following road No. 83 from its junction with road No. 81 about 3 miles from Highway 90. Turn right again onto road No. 8312 in another 2.8 miles. Views from the top.

This road may be closed at times during the summer. Good views of the mountain, however, even if you can't make it to the top.

The closest view of St. Helens from this side of the mountain.

Nearest camping

Cougar, Kalama Springs, Swift

Curly Creek Falls and Natural Bridge

78   NATURAL BRIDGE

Pick your own way to a small delicate natural bridge, or hike up a quiet river.

From the St. Helens Ranger Station continue easterly on Highway 90, taking fork to the right .2 mile beyond the ranger station. The road follows the Lewis River north into the Mt. Adams country near Baby Shoe Pass.

Highway 90 also links with road No. 51 (5.4 miles from the ranger station) leading into the Wind River country.

NATURAL BRIDGE

A small eroded arch in the middle of a frenzied little stairstep waterfalls on Curly Creek just above the Lewis River.

Difficult to find. No trails. But one of the most delicate and intimate attractions in the area. (It may be flooded by another reservoir planned on the upper Lewis River.)

For cross-river views of the arch and another falls further down the river, drive past Curly Creek about .8 mile turning left (north) onto road No. 9039. Park on the far (north) side of the Lewis River bridge and then hike down the north bank of the river (to the west). Arch falls in about .3 mile. Hike another quarter mile to a second cross-river falls on Miller Creek.

For a view down the falls and over the heavily eroded stream bed above the falls, drive easterly beyond the ranger station on 90 to Curly Creek, 4.3 miles, then backtrack to the first clearcut below the road, less than .25 mile.

Park on the road and follow the fireline around the edge of the clearcut, on the Curly Creek side, downhill toward the Lewis River. Turn right toward Curly Creek on a ridge above the river where the clearcut fireline starts bearing left. Watch for possible tag-line plastic markers.

Do **NOT** go over the ridge to the river (on this route). Keeping **above** the river, pick your way along the ridge carefully toward Curly Creek to the right. ⚐

Find the small, table-size natural bridge below a small waterfall. (Curly Creek plunges over another falls into the river.) Use care in approaching the falls on slippery rock. Also note the many eroded bowls in the upper creek bed and how the rock "floor" below the first falls has been etched full of grating-like holes.

No place for children or the unwary.

LEWIS RIVER TRAIL

A quiet trail along the Lewis River that goes just about as far as you want to walk it. Bolt Camp shelter in 2.2 miles.

Turn left off 90 onto road No. 9039 about 5.1 miles from the St. Helens Ranger Station and beyond Curly Creek (see above). Road No. 9039 drops to a log-stringer bridge across the Lewis River.

To find trail turn right onto the first logging spur road beyond the bridge. Parking and trail sign.

Trail drops down to the river and then wends upstream to the shelter and beyond. Petrified wood is often found near the river. Otherwise it's simply a pleasant place for a slow and easy walk. ⚐

Nearest camping

Swift, Clearwater

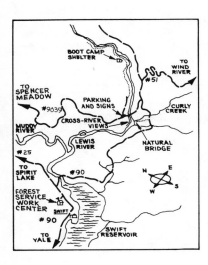

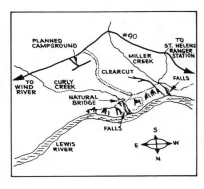

X SOUTH ST. HELENS

79 SPENCER MEADOWS

Quiet, clear views of Adams and St. Helens over boggy meadows surrounded by timber.

From the St. Helens Ranger Station continue easterly on 90, forking left in about .2 mile onto No. 25, continuing on road No. 25 across the Muddy River, turning right onto road No. 93 in about .3 mile from the Muddy River bridge.

Follow "Spencer Meadow" signs on road No. 93. Butte area in about 12 miles from the 25/93 junction.

Views of Mt. Adams to the east off upper reaches of the road. St. Helens to the west. Caution: Heavy logging traffic during the week.

SPENCER BUTTE

Hike 1.5 miles to the top of Spencer Butte at 4247 feet for views of St. Helens, Adams, Hood, and Jefferson.

Drive 8.3 miles to the first trail on the left and 11.3 miles to the second from the 25/93 junction. Both trails lead to the former lookout site atop the butte in 1.5 miles. Hike up one and back the other.

Trails start out in open timber and then climb to huckleberry meadows for views out at the big peaks, down on the meadows, and up the Lewis River and Clear Creek drainage basins.

SPENCER MEADOWS

Watch for elk at dawn or dusk over meadows with views toward both Adams and St. Helens.

From the 25/93 junction drive about 11.7 miles to the Spencer Meadow sign on road No. 93. Or for better views drive up a short spur road — beginning of the northern Spencer Butte Trail (see above). Road leads to a primitive camp area in less than .25 mile.

Prowl open meadows for bog-type flowers, birds, and glimpses of game. If you camp, bring water. 🛏

SPENCER BUTTE ARCH

Hike to an arch perched on the side of a mountain with views of St. Helens in addition.

To find the arch, hike to the top of Spencer Butte (see above) and then make your way cross-country to the west from the site of the old lookout (watch for debris).

No trail here, so make your way carefully downhill about .25 mile, watching as you go. But don't go over the brow of the hill — cliffs and dangers — until you've spotted the arch.

It's well worth looking for. ↑

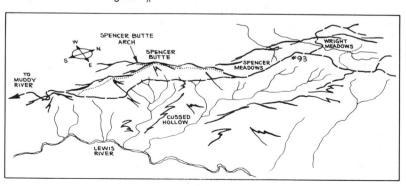

Cotton-grass at Spencer Meadows

Nearest camping
    Swift, Clearwater, Primitive camps in open meadows. No facilities.

Y SPIRIT LAKE

It will be a long, long time before the slopes of St. Helens grow back to the beauty that existed before the mountain erupted May 18, 1980.

But you can watch the progress nature is making — and look back on the damage she did — from a network of viewpoints and roads being constructed in the 110,000-acre Mount St. Helens National Volcanic Monument.

To reach the vista points and trailheads, either drive south from Randle on forest road No. 25 or east from Woodland on state highway 503 to Yale Lake, Swift Reservoir, and road No. 25.

Forest roads here may be closed, particularly on weekdays, by construction and logging. Check at ranger stations or information centers.

Camping and hiking are permitted throughout the monument, except in formally restricted areas, subject to the usual Forest Service regulations.

Two warnings. First, don't drink or even touch the water in this area. It may contain high concentrations of potentially dangerous micro-organisms. Second, be aware of the heat dangers in summer. With no shade, the area can be as hot as a desert, so carry water and protect yourself and your pets from the sun.

Formal viewpoints and trails (scheduled for completion in 1983):

1. Ryan Lake Interpretive Site — View of blast area and effects on Ryan Lake area. (See also page 159.)
2. Strawberry Viewpoint — View of

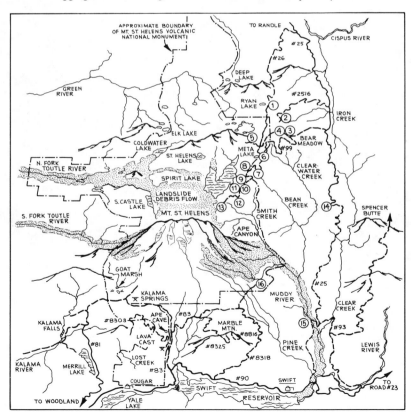

Spirit Lake and St. Helens from near Independence Pass viewpoint

St. Helens, blast area, and lava dome. Short trail to viewpoint.

3. Bear Meadow Viewpoints — View of St. Helens from Rosenquist photo point. Picnicking, rest rooms, and trailhead for Boundary Trail.

4. Boundary Trail (Bear Meadow to Bismark Pass) — View of volcano-blasted timber, both downed and standing.

5. Boundary Trail (Bismark Pass to Norway Pass) — Two-mile trail with view from Norway Pass of Spirit Lake, St. Helens, debris flow, and blast area.

6. Meta Lake Interpretive Site — Blast area, wrecked automobile, and short trail to Meta Lake.

7. Volcano View — St. Helens and headwaters of Smith and Bean Creeks.

8. Independence Pass Trail and Viewpoint — Quarter-mile trail to Independence Pass with view of Spirit Lake, St. Helens, Mt. Margaret, debris dam, and blast area.

9. Harmony Viewpoint — View of Spirit Lake, Mt. Margaret, and blast area.

10. Cedar Creek Viewpoint — View of Spirit Lake, Mt. Margaret, St. Helens, and blast area.

11. Donnybrook Viewpoint — Spirit Lake, debris flow, Mt. Margaret, and blast area.

12. Smith Creek Viewpoint — View of Smith Creek drainage, east side of St. Helens, and blast area.

13. View Ridge Viewpoint — Spirit Lake, debris flow, St. Helens, Mt. Margaret, and blast area.

14. Clearwater Overlook — Clearwater panorama including blast area and timber salvage.

15. Muddy River Mudflow — Interpretive site with view of Muddy River mudflow.

16. Lava Canyon Interpretive Site —Short trail to view of shoestring mudflow.

Multnomah Falls

Z COLUMBIA RIVER

This grand river deserves all of the volumes written about it. And its story is still being told.

The great dams illustrate modern man's attempts to tame the river, while the cliffs and waterfalls along its shores demonstrate nature's resistance to change. The few samplings listed here will provide just a glimpse of both its "developments" and original beauties.

Drive east from Vancouver on Highway 14 to the toll bridge at Cascade Locks, returning to Portland on I-84 and the Old Columbia River Highway. Take a full day, at least. More if you have the time.

CAMPGROUNDS
Beacon Rock State Park — 35 sites on a loop away from the highway. Restrooms. Piped water. Boat launching and fishing. Fee.

Eagle Creek — 20 sites on a forest bluff above the Columbia. Drive east on I-84 turning right just beyond the Bonneville turnoff. (From the west, leave I-84 at Bonneville Dam, looping back onto the freeway, eastbound, turning off again in about a mile. Flush toilets. Piped water.

Ainsworth — 45 sites on a grassy loop just off the old highway about 3.5 miles west of Multnomah Falls. Flush toilets. Piped water. Fee.

Viento — 63 sites on open slopes. 8 miles west of Hood River on I-84. Flush toilets. Piped water. Fee.

Wyeth — 17 sites including family sites. Just off I-84 from the Wyeth interchange about 5 miles east of Cascade Locks. Restrooms. Piped water. Fee.

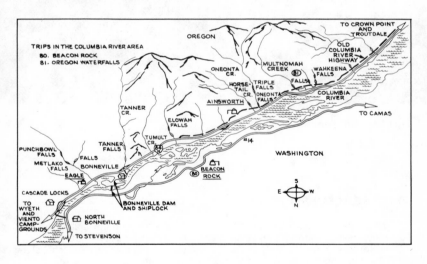

Trail to top of Beacon Rock

80 BEACON ROCK

Climb 52 switchbacks, crossing 22 bridges, to look down on the Columbia River. Take other trails to waterfalls and even higher views from Hamilton Mountain.

Drive south from Seattle on Highway 5 to Vancouver and then 35 miles east along the Columbia River on Highway 14 to Beacon Rock State Park.

Find trail to the top of 848-foot Beacon Rock off parking areas to the right of the highway. Trail starts to the right of the restroom and climbs 52 short switchbacks up the face of the rock above the river. Viewpoint at the top in .9 mile. You will probably have lots of company. Over 10,000 people hike the trail every year.

Find trails to Rodney and Hardy Falls and to Little Hamilton and Hamilton Mountains out of both campground and picnic loops off park road to the left of the highway. 3 miles to the top of Hamilton Mountain from the picnic area; **Rodney** and **Hardy Falls** in 1.5 miles on Hardy Creek. Note Pool of Winds, a large basin scoured in rock, below Rodney Falls.

Trail switchbacks steeply above the falls to a trail junction below **Little Hamilton.** Take trail fork, left, to the next spur in another half-mile, turning right for views from

Little Hamilton. Continue on main trail, up still more switchbacks, for views from **Hamilton Mountain** at 2432 feet.

Other trails from campground and picnic loops lead along Little Creek to Little Beacon Rock. Watch for signs.

Nearest camping
Beacon Rock State Park

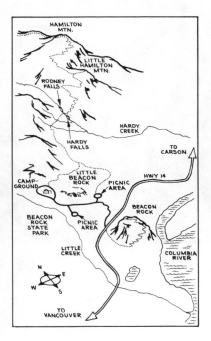

Hamilton Mountain trail

Rooster Rock

81 OREGON WATERFALLS

In just one short section of the Columbia River Gorge, on the Oregon side of the river, dozens of spectacular waterfalls. Some can be seen from the highway. But many others are reserved for those willing to hike down short forest trails.

Find the falls south of the Old Columbia River highway, a pleasant-to-drive spur road off freeway I-84 between Portland and Cascade Locks.

From Portland turn off I-84 at Troutdale. From Cascade Locks turn off the freeway 5 miles west of Bonneville.

MULTNOMAH FALLS

One of the most spectacular falls in the west. And certainly one of the most popular. More than 2 million visitors a year. Yet you can escape the hustle of crowds by hiking any of the nearby trails.

Either follow the old highway east of Troutdale to the recreation complex below the falls. Or turn off I-84 at the Multnomah Falls interchange.

For best view of the 620-foot torrent just follow the crowds to any of the viewpoints south of the highway. Try them all.

For a scenic loop hike from the base of the falls to the top of it and then on down to Wahkeena Falls and back again, take the trail uphill from the east side of the bridge below the falls.

The trail climbs first to the top of the falls in 1 mile. A grind, but worth the effort. Cross Multnomah Creek and then turn right onto the Perdition Trail, following it downhill to the foot of Wahkeena Falls, its parking area and a trail that returns to Multnomah. A 2-mile round trip.

But don't pass up the marked spur trails to spectacular vista points at the top of the falls and about .3 mile off the Perdition Trail after you start downhill.

Other trails and other loops, if you've got the time.

ONEONTA and HORSETAIL

First look into a tiny, fern-draped gorge and then hike above it to four waterfalls. A 3.8-mile round trip.

Find the pretty gorge south of the old highway about 2.2 miles east of Multnomah Falls. No trail here, but you can walk up the creek when the water is low.

Find the trail to the waterfalls from a parking lot west of the small gorge. First hike uphill to the top of Triple Falls and then back to a side trail (east) which passes Oneonta, Ponytail and Horsetail Falls. Return to your car along the highway.

PUNCH BOWL

A rock bowl full of waterfalls in about 2 miles with an appetizer along the way.

Find the trailhead at the end of the road along the creek in the Eagle Creek Picnic Area (see Eagle Creek Campground).

The path climbs 1.5 miles to a short trail (right) to Metalko Falls and then on, in another half-mile to a viewpoint above Punch Bowl Falls.

CROWN POINT

Sorry, no waterfalls. But one of the easiest and grandest vistas in the Columbia Gorge. All from a classic, domed building perched on the edge of a cliff.

From Troutdale, drive east on the old highway as it climbs to vistas and the scenic park. 25 miles east of Portland.

Nearest camping

Eagle Creek, Ainsworth State Park, Viento State Park, Wyeth

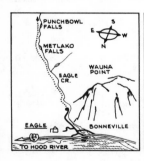
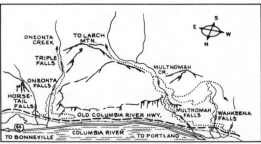

READING SUGGESTIONS

Readers may find the following books helpful in gaining a fuller understanding of the outdoors.

FLOWERS

Trees, Shrubs, and Flowers to Know in Washington, C. P. Lyon. J. M. Dent and Sons, Ltd., Vancouver, B.C., Canada.

101 Wildflowers of Mount Rainier National Park, Grant and Wenonah Sharpe. University of Washington Press, Seattle.

Vascular Plants of the Pacific Northwest, Hitchcock, Cronquist, Owenby, and Thompson. 5 vols. University of Washington Press, Seattle.

Mountain Flowers, Harvey Manning and Bob and Ira Spring. The Mountaineers, Seattle.

SEASHORE

The Edge of the Sea, Rachel Carson. Houghton Mifflin Co., Boston.

The Olympic Seashore, Ruth Kirk. Olympic Natural History Association, Port Angeles, Wash.

Between Pacific Tides, Edward Rickets and Jack Calvin. Stanford University Press, Palo Alto, Calif.

Animals of the Seashore, Muriel Guberlet. Binfords and Mort, Portland, Ore.

Seaweeds at Ebbtide, Muriel Guberlet. University of Washington Press, Seattle.

NATURE GUIDES

A Field Guide to Western Birds, Roger Tory Peterson. Houghton Mifflin Company, Boston.

A Field Guide to the Mammals, William H. Burt and Richard P. Grossenheider. Houghton Mifflin Company, Boston.

A Field Guide to Animal Tracks, Olaus J. Murie. Houghton Mifflin Company, Boston.

A Field Guide to the Ferns, Boughton Cobb. Houghton Mifflin Company, Boston.

Field Book of Nature Activities and Conservation, William Hillcourt. Putnam and Sons, New York.

Insects, Ross E. Hutchins. Prentice-Hall, Inc., Englewood Cliffs, N.J.

Plants and Animals of the Pacific Northwest, Eugene N. Kozloff. University of Washington Press, Seattle.

Animal Tracks of the Pacific Northwest, Karen Pandell and Chris Stall. The Mountaineers, Seattle.

GEOLOGY

Scenic Geology of the Pacific Northwest, Leonard C. Ekman. Binfords and Mort, Portland, Ore.

Principles of Geology, James Gilluly, A.C. Waters, and A.O. Woodford. W.H. Freeman and Co., San Francisco.

Origin of Cascade Landscapes, J. Hoover Mackin and Allen S. Cares. Div. Mines and Geology Ind. Circ. No. 41, Washington State Department of Conservation, Olympia.

Routes and Rocks, Hiker's Guide to the North Cascades from Glacier Peak to Lake Chelan, D.F. Crowder and R.W. Tabor. The Mountaineers, Seattle.

Elements of Geology, James W. Zumberge. John Wiley and Sons, Inc., New York.

Exploring Glaciers with a Camera, A.E. Harrison. The Sierra Club, San Francisco.

Caves of Washington, William R. Halliday. Washington Department of Conservation, Division of Mines and Geology, Olympia.

Fire and Ice, The Cascade Volcanoes, Stephen L. Harris. The Mountaineers and Pacific Search, Seattle.

Guide to the Geology of Olympic National Park, Rowland W. Tabor. University of Washington Press, Seattle.

MUSHROOMS

The Savory Wild Mushroom, Margaret McKenny. University of Washington Press, Seattle.

Mushroom Hunter's Field Guide, Alexander H. Smith. University of Michigan Press, Ann Arbor, Mich.

WILDERNESS TRAVEL

Mountaineering, The Freedom of the Hills, Fourth Edition, Ed Peters, editor. The Mountaineers, Seattle.

Backpacking: One Step at a Time, Harvey Manning. REI Press, Seattle.

CONSERVATION

Wild Cascades: Forgotten Parkland, Harvey Manning. The Sierra Club, San Francisco.

My Wilderness: The Pacific West, William O. Douglas. Doubleday and Company, Inc., Garden City, N.Y.

The North Cascades, Tom Miller and Harvey Manning. The Mountaineers, Seattle.

A Sand County Almanac, Aldo Leopold. Oxford University Press, New York.

Steep Trails, John Muir. Houghton Mifflin Company, New York.

The South Cascades: The Gifford Pinchot National Forest, E.M. Sterling. The Mountaineers, Seattle.

GUIDES

50 Hikes in Mount Rainier National Park, Spring and Manning. The Mountaineers, Seattle.

Exploring Mount Rainier, Ruth Kirk. University of Washington Press, Seattle.

Cascade Alpine Guide, Climbing and High Routes, Columbia River to Stevens Pass, Fred Beckey. The Mountaineers, Seattle.

Climbers Guide to the Olympic Mountains, Olympic Mountain Rescue. The Mountaineers, Seattle.

PLACES TO CALL OR WRITE FOR INFORMATION AND MAPS

Information on the conditions of roads and trails can be obtained at the following headquarter and district offices of the Forest Service and National Park Service.

Maps can be obtained at ranger stations or by writing Forest Supervisors at headquarter offices. The National Park Service offers a brochure showing roads and major trails in each national park.

SNOQUALMIE NATIONAL FOREST
Information, Mt. Baker-Snoqualmie National Forest, 1018 First Avenue, Seattle, Wash. 98104.

WENATCHEE NATIONAL FOREST
Headquarters, P.O. Building, Box 811, Wenatchee, Wash. 98801.
Naches-Tieton Ranger Station, Naches, Wash. 98937.

GIFFORD PINCHOT NATIONAL FOREST
Headquarters, 500 W. 12th St., Vancouver, Wash. 98660.
St. Helens Ranger Station, Amboy, Wash. 98601.
Mt. Adams Ranger Station, Trout Lake, Wash. 98650.
Packwood Ranger Station, Packwood, Wash. 98361.
Randle Ranger Station, Randle, Wash. 98377.
Wind River Ranger Station, Carson, Wash. 98610.

MOUNT RAINIER NATIONAL PARK
Headquarters, Longmire, Wash. 98397.

OLYMPIC NATIONAL PARK
Headquarters, Ashford, Wash. 98304

REGIONAL OFFICE, NATIONAL PARK SERVICE
2001 Sixth Avenue, Seattle, Wash. 98121.